NOBODY REMEMBERS SECOND

Aston Villa 1989-1993

RICHARD SYDENHAM

pitch

First published by Pitch Publishing, 2024

Pitch Publishing
9 Donnington Park,
85 Birdham Road,
Chichester, West Sussex,
PO20 7AJ
www.pitchpublishing.co.uk
info@pitchpublishing.co.uk

A CIP catalogue record is available for this book from the British Library.

ISBN 978 1 80150 760 8

MIX
Paper | Supporting responsible forestry
FSC® C013604

Printed and bound in the UK on FSC® certified paper in line with our continuing commitment to ethical business practices, sustainability and the environment.

Typesetting and origination by Pitch Publishing
Printed and bound by CPI Anthony Rowe, UK

Contents

Thanks to my mum and dad, Linda and Derek, for always being there for me. It was Dad who took me and my brother Jeff to Villa Park, first for £1.50 through the old Holte End 'Juveniles' turnstiles when adult prices were still £3. Saturday afternoons were always about going to Villa Park, from as early as I can recall. Dad's best mates – Viv Wilson, and the late Brian Ward and Gordon Calcutt – were like unofficial uncles to me and the camaraderie of seeing them all playing cards (usually Crash) in the pub on matchdays, while discussing the team and such like, were good days that I look back on fondly.

Thanks also to the Villa family who still want to learn more about the club's history, which makes writing these books worthwhile. I hope you enjoy this latest reflection of Villa's past.

The Villa family, of course, includes those no longer with us such as former players of this era who we all knew and admired from the terraces, including Dalian Atkinson, Cyrille Regis, Paul Birch, Bernie Gallacher, Ugo Ehiogu, Les Sealey and Gary Shaw who were all taken far too early.

And, finally, thanks to the one and only Gordon 'Sid' Cowans. In terms of the period I have focused on in these pages, he was instrumental in the 1989/90 season under Graham Taylor and returned to Villa for a third spell in 1993/94. Gordon has been having a few challenges in recent times, and I know the Villa family will share my best wishes to him. Never mind his class as a player, I will never forget his generosity when he contributed to and helped me to promote my last book on Villa, *Ticket to the Moon*. I know he'd love this book, too. Quality player, quality man.

Author's Note

MY LAST book on Aston Villa, *Ticket to the Moon*, focused exhaustively on the 1970s and 1980s and detailed a fascinating rise and fall journey around the club's golden era.

I was drawn to writing *this* latest book, though, not because it's the most successful era in Villa's history, but because I have lost count of the amount of people who tell me it was their *favourite* time watching Villa.

Graham Taylor and Ron Atkinson are often cited by supporters as being two of Villa's best or most popular managers. Their teams so nearly won the English top division, which would have crowned Villa as champions twice in four seasons – but of course they didn't. As good and worthy as both teams were as potential champions in 1989/90 and 1992/93, they ultimately wilted on the home straight. And as we all know in this ruthless world of sport, nobody remembers second. But it's my job here to hopefully ensure these teams do have something of a legacy in print.

The unfulfilled promise is impossible to deny; it happened. However, it doesn't mean their near-misses are not a good story worth telling. Why did Villa falter on both occasions and why were these amazing seasons sandwiched between relegation dogfights or mediocrity?

There are fascinating contrasts in this period that also saw English football's first foreign manager appointed when Jozef Vengloš took up chairman Doug Ellis's offer to take charge of Aston Villa.

Although I was first introduced to Villa in the title-winning season of 1980/81, I was still only approaching my seventh birthday then and therefore such memories are distant. I probably enjoyed the 1989/90 season under Graham Taylor's management more than any other.

I find it curious that Taylor held on, somewhat unfairly, to the reputation that his teams played long-ball, direct or boring football. To me, that is a lazy analysis of Taylor's work. He probably did play that brand of football at times at Watford when his playing resources were not as rich as they became at Villa, and latterly England. He relied on a solid defence at

Vicarage Road and talented forwards such as John Barnes and Luther Blissett. At Villa, Taylor and his excellent coaching staff were responsible for some of the most vibrant football I have ever seen at Villa Park. Again, based on a sound defence led by the genius that was Paul McGrath, he had the pace of Tony Daley, the craft and creativity of an experienced Gordon Cowans, and goals from an up-and-coming David Platt, after rampaging striker Alan McInally had left.

The best compliment I can pay to Ron Atkinson is that after a difficult season under Venglоš that almost resulted in relegation, he came in and made Villa supporters believe again.

With the signature strut and confidence of a two-time FA Cup-winning boss at Manchester United, he was a master at signing established, quality players that many cynical but realistic supporters deemed 'too good for Villa'. The way he charmed the likes of Dean Saunders, Andy Townsend, Steve Staunton, Ray Houghton and others to Villa Park lifted morale and subsequently raised expectation levels when they were low.

Big Ron wasn't anti-youth, either. He recruited Mark Bosnich and Ugo Ehiogu as rookies and encouraged the development of players like Dwight Yorke, Steve Froggatt, Bryan Small and Graham Fenton. Like Taylor, his work deserved all the positive recognition that came his way.

It's only a shame this story doesn't end with the fairy tale of a league title win. But Villa came mighty close, and at least there was a League Cup triumph in '94 to cap some kind of success.

Richard Sydenham

Worcestershire, August 2024

Foreword by Dwight Yorke

WHEN I arrived at Aston Villa in 1989, I was just so impressed that I had been recruited by such an iconic football club. It was my first trip to Europe, my first experience as a professional and learning about life in England. Life was a bit of a blur in the early days as I got used to the weather, the people, the culture, everything.

It was a new world to me and I learned quite a lot in those first few months, especially from those three iconic players Paul McGrath, who was idolised by the Villa players and fans; David Platt, who was a god in his own right – he was on the up and heading for greatness and I learned a lot from his work ethic; and then there was Sid Cowans, the father figure who everyone appreciated for his experience, the silkiness of his skills and passing ability, and his vision to create. Then you had the nitty-gritty of players like Kent Nielsen and Derek Mountfield; Nigel Spink, who had been part of the furniture at Villa for so long; and then Tony Daley, who was like a big brother to me. I was very lucky to have these guys around me as I was in the infancy of my footballing education, and it was important I developed quickly.

I was around the squad when we were runners-up in 1989/90, but having made just two appearances as a sub, I felt the disappointment of not winning the league a lot more in the 1992/93 season under Big Ron.

I matured a lot in those early years as I had gone from having the father figure of Graham Taylor nurturing me in my first few months at the club, to the soft-spoken, caring Jozef Vengloš who was interested in my development, to Big Ron [laughs], with his arrogance of having been there and done it, his suntan, his bling Rolex watch and all that sort of stuff, which was great. You always knew what he wanted and expected of you.

Make no mistake, we were good enough to have won the league and having played at Villa for the best part of a decade I can now look back and reflect that it was a typical Villa mentality, to think that getting so close to being champions is good enough. I understand why those mentalities exist.

I hate to say it but having played at Villa and then at Manchester United, that was the difference that separated us. Coming second at Villa was acceptable, I think. It wasn't hurtful enough for us at the time. The attitude was kind of like, 'Winning the league will be great, but if we don't, we've still done well.'

I loved winning the League Cup with Villa in 1996 and scoring at Wembley against Leeds United in front of our fantastic supporters. It's still a medal I cherish. But don't let anybody tell you any different that a league title is the big prize. Nobody remembers second, that's true. I went to United and experienced a different level of winning mentality. Second is acceptable at so many clubs but not for the serial winners. Look at the Arsenal supporters in recent times, boasting that they pushed Manchester City all the way and only narrowly lost the title. But at the end of the day, they will be forgotten about for coming second, which is exactly what happened to us at Villa in '93. We were a very good team and had a chance to make history, which is what you play the game for. You want to go back to Villa Park and have people say, 'He won the league, and this trophy and that trophy.' That's why I left Villa, not because I didn't love the club, because I do and always will – it was a big part of my life. But as a player with ambition, you want to win league titles and I had to go to United to do that.

Because of the decision I made I feel I don't get the credit [I deserve] at Villa when I go back there. There's a different feeling towards other players who also left the football club to further their careers like Jack Grealish, Ashley Young, Gareth Barry and many others. Nobody wore that Villa shirt with more pride than me. I gave almost ten years to Villa, and I had a quite incredible time there. I only left because I felt I had given everything I possibly could and wanted to challenge myself on another level. I get a bit bemused and distressed by the negative legacy I seem to have with a section of Villa supporters. The famous John Gregory quote when I left didn't help me, as it stirred the fans up, but there is no way that if John had the opportunity to have been the Manchester United manager, he would have turned it down. I know he would have left in the same way.

Ultimately, Villa will always have a big place in my heart and my memories and it's just a real shame that we didn't go that step further in those two seasons.

Dwight Yorke

Dubai, July 2024

Foreword by Nigel Spink

'We probably blew it if we're honest with ourselves and faded away with some poor results that should have been better, especially at both ends of the season'

IT WAS always going to be hard for me to better *'that'* night in Rotterdam in 1982, but in hindsight it was a real shame we couldn't go one better in our league campaigns under Graham Taylor and Ron Atkinson when Villa twice finished runners-up (in 1990 and 1993).

When Aston Villa won the league in '81, I spent the whole season in the reserves as Jimmy Rimmer's deputy, so this was now my time to win the league.

Initially, it was an interesting time for the club having been promoted back into the old First Division (in 1988), and only narrowly going up ahead of other clubs.

Then we had an awful start back in the top flight and just managed to stay up.

But under Graham there was a philosophy that didn't change. He didn't panic and seemed to have a plan for us. He was a genius with tactics. I vividly recall how he came into training one day with the idea of playing big Sticks (Ian Ormondroyd) out wide because he wasn't strong in the air. Training, tactics and attitudes all remained the same and the only thing that did change was the playing personnel as he brought in players like Paul McGrath and Kent Nielsen.

Paul McGrath – what a player! In the first game I played with him, I remember he ran towards the touchline for a challenge and just belted the ball into Row Z. He then jogged back to get into position, and he looked at me and said, 'They won't fuckin' score from up there!' He had all the quality in the world, but he also knew when to keep it simple. He was great on the ball but didn't take chances.

It didn't surprise me that we challenged for the league in that 1989/90 season because Graham had created an environment that was built for that kind of target.

The 6-2 win over Everton is the result that people remember most and I would say it was the game where everything just clicked and felt like we were on to something. You need results like that to give you the belief, and they were a fine side as well and were shell-shocked by what we did to them. The balance of the team was brilliant with Macca (Paul McGrath), Platty (David Platt) and Sid (Gordon Cowans) the standouts.

As a group of lads, we had a good camaraderie and social scene together as well, maybe the best since the early eighties, so things were working on and off the field.

We probably blew it if we're honest with ourselves and faded away with some poor results that should have been better, especially at both ends of the season. Liverpool were, ultimately, stronger than us, but we had our chances. Still, second is nothing to be ashamed of.

Dr Jo's one season was a difficult time for us as he clearly didn't work out. Ron Atkinson was probably what we needed afterwards as he brought a bounce and a confidence that we were crying out for. He went for the high-profile signings and most of them worked well.

Big Ron's tenure was the beginning of the end for me though, as Mark Bosnich came in when I got injured. Ron then preferred him from there on. Bozzy was like Ron in his character, flamboyant and outgoing, so Ron took to him. But to be fair to Bozzy he was a fine goalkeeper, he was a big presence in the goal and made some amazing saves.

In the end, we let another title go begging as Man United didn't slip up like we did. We faded towards the end of both seasons and I guess ended up with what we deserved because of those inconsistencies. It wasn't to be.

Nigel Spink

Lichfield, September 2024

‘I always say, “First is first, second is nowhere.” Maybe that is a bit unfair when you’re talking about the league, but nobody remembers people who come second very often.’

Andy Gray
Warwickshire, May 2024

1

Revival, Then Survival

'Taylor ruthlessly advised club legend Andy Gray that he was going to move him on before embarking on a tough promotion bid. He did not wish to compete with Gray's robust personality in the dressing room. There would only be room for one boss and one leader, and he wanted that to be himself.'

GRAHAM TAYLOR'S journey to becoming Aston Villa manager was slightly ironic and included a few twists of fate. He first became aware of Villa's interest in him in the summer of 1987 while he was at Watford. Word had reached him from the former Villa manager Dick Taylor, who was then selling training kit to clubs for his sports shop business, based near Villa Park.

Curiously, the Hornets boss had first set eyes on Dick Taylor when he was a schoolboy as Dick underwent training runs past his house while playing for Scunthorpe United in the 1950s. Graham was the son of a sports journalist on the *Scunthorpe Evening Telegraph* at the time. Fast forward more than three decades and Graham would become Villa boss, a position which Dick held from 1964 to 1967.

Graham filled the position vacated by Billy McNeill, the Scotland and Celtic legend who had been fired by chairman Doug Ellis after eight torrid months in charge at Villa. McNeill suffered the ignominy of helping to relegate Villa and his former club Manchester City to the Second Division in the same miserable season, 1986/87.

Taylor soon learned that Ellis was a more controlling, hands-on chairman than he had become used to from working with pop-star owner Elton John at Vicarage Road. Nonetheless, Taylor possessed the intelligence to cajole Ellis and allow him the egotistical space he needed but he was in total command of the area he was interested in, namely football matters.

When Taylor signed on at Villa Park, it was he who was taking a chance as he was leaving a comfortable job at a top-flight club to drop down a division to manage a team that badly needed reorganising and reshaping to earn promotion and achieve future success. It was a gamble he was happy to take and which subsequently paid dividends for him, even if Ellis had refused to match the salary that Watford were paying him and also denied him the use of a Jaguar car that he had become accustomed to.

Taylor immersed himself in all things Villa. He gleaned, from reading the local papers, that the supporters held the penny-pinching Ellis responsible for the relegation, and not so much the two managers who had presided over the dreadful season, McNeill and Graham Turner.

Taylor was quick to assemble a staff he was familiar with. He hired Steve Harrison as first-team coach, Jim Walker as physio and Bobby Downes as his youth coach, while Dave Richardson returned to Villa from Leicester City.

The playing personnel also required surgery. Some business had been agreed before Taylor's arrival as Paul Elliott (to Pisa) and Tony Dorigo (to Chelsea) had committed to leave Villa. Mercurial winger Mark Walters soon followed them out the door to Rangers, for a fee of £700,000 that bolstered the new manager's transfer kitty. Taylor's first signings were a central defender he knew well at Watford, Steve Sims, and striker Alan McInally from Celtic. He had agreed to sign McInally for Watford but once he took the Villa job, he derailed that move and secured McInally's services for his new club, albeit for an extra £100,000 as the Celtic chairman shrewdly noted that Villa was a bigger club. McInally, who Villa fans nicknamed 'Rambo', had been in the shadows, somewhat, of Brian McClair and Mo Johnston at Celtic and was now ready to make his name.

'When I came to Aston Villa they really were in turmoil,' McInally recalled. 'They were in such a difficult position when they got relegated. They had players in the team who weren't good enough to play for Aston Villa. Graham Taylor knew he had to bring in better players than what they had and players who would fight for the badge.'

Taylor ruthlessly advised club legend Andy Gray that he was going to move him on before embarking on a tough promotion bid. He did not wish to compete with Gray's robust personality in the dressing room. There would only be room for one boss and one leader, and he wanted that to be himself. Gray was annoyed that he wasn't given the chance to show he could be a leader on the manager's side rather than against him, but nonetheless found a new home at nearby West Brom.

'Andy was very popular at Villa Park because of his first spell at the club, but I felt he had too much influence around the place,' Taylor commented. 'Don't get me wrong, I liked Andy, but I needed to demonstrate that I was the boss and that it was not optional to follow my rules.

'Andy was 31 and had been at the top and I felt I needed players who had a hunger and desire to get there rather than someone who had been there already.'

Taylor's last quip on Gray was refreshingly honest but slightly contradictory when he also signed Derek Mountfield, who had experienced the same success at Everton that Gray had; while Nigel Spink and Allan Evans (and Gordon Cowans who he signed subsequently) had won the European Cup at Villa, and Paul McGrath was an established international and an FA Cup winner at Manchester United. The former explanation was clearly the biggest reason for Gray's departure.

Another Andy Gray then arrived, in the shape of the Crystal Palace midfielder, and his namesake Stuart, from Barnsley. Attacking midfielder Mark

Lillis joined from Derby County where he had struggled for game time, while Notts County legend David Hunt also added depth to a new-look Villa midfield that included Paul Birch, Steve Hunt and Andy Blair.

European Cup winner Gary Williams left for Leeds United after almost a decade at Villa Park and one of his replacements at right-back (Taylor also signed Chris Price from Blackburn Rovers) was Kevin Gage from Wimbledon. It wasn't long before Taylor was exploiting Gage's versatility and playing him in the centre of midfield and even at left-back sometimes.

'Once I went to Villa Park and walked around the place and met everybody, it was a no-brainer that I'd be signing for them even though I was dropping down a division to do so,' Gage said. 'Wimbledon had just finished sixth in the old First Division, but we were massively punching above our weight with an average gate of around 6,000. Taylor sold Aston Villa to me, and I didn't need much persuading. He explained that Villa did not intend on staying down in that league for very long and that my experience of promotions with Wimbledon would be very important to his Villa project.

'Wimbledon tried to match what Villa were paying me but even if they had offered me the world, I had my heart set on leaving for Villa. I saw the potential at Villa, and I was also keen to work under Graham after what he had achieved at Watford.'

Stuart Gray also signed for Villa largely based on Taylor's reputation. He quickly observed why players enjoyed working for the manager. Not only did he feel Taylor was organised and tactically astute, but he saw an empathy towards players that many other managers did not possess.

'Graham took the trouble of coming to my home with his wife, Rita,' Gray recalled. 'He spoke to me for about 20 minutes and everything he promised he would do, he delivered on. So, to then have the privilege of him making me the Aston Villa captain made it even more special. My first room-mate was Allan Evans and he was such a great ambassador and captain of Villa and I could see what the club meant to him. So, for me to follow someone like Allan as captain, who was a top pro and a great bloke, meant a great deal.'

Evans, meanwhile, was certainly not bitter at his ousting as skipper. On the contrary – he was enjoying the fresh, positive environment that Taylor and his staff had created.

'I know that Graham brought in Steve Sims to replace me but that motivated me and I soon found that the defensive techniques being shown to us in training by Steve Harrison were almost revolutionary,' Evans said. 'I learned more about the art of defending in my one season under Graham and his staff than I had in my previous ten years at Villa.'

Taylor's home debut was against Birmingham City. Quite a baptism. It was on that day he grasped the strength of feeling, or hatred, between the two clubs and realised it was much worse than the Watford versus Luton encounters he had previously viewed as being a bit tasty. This was another level. Blues won 2-0 and the result invited some early pressure on the new manager. In fact, they were 19th in the Second Division after his first month in charge. But the more his influence impacted the players, the better results became.

Taylor gradually found the right balance with which to humour Ellis, like when he had to listen to the story of how he invented the bicycle kick when in Tranmere Rovers' reserves. There were many more, as the manager listened and smiled politely when others might have ended such anecdotes a little more abruptly and rudely.

Taylor drove back to Vicarage Road a couple of times during that first season at Villa, not to meet old friends, but just to remind himself of the happy times he had had at Watford, which was the town where his daughters had grown up. It was not a case of self-doubt, but more a way of reminding himself of why he took on the ambitious challenge of Villa.

Another month into his first season, Villa were sixth and on their way towards an eventual promotion, as runners-up to Millwall. The Londoners finished four points ahead, while Villa pipped Middlesbrough to the second automatic promotion place by virtue of superior goals scored, despite the same points (78), and same goal difference (+27).

Taylor's first objective was complete: promotion, tick.

Along the way that season, Steve Harrison left Taylor's staff to make his first move into management by taking the Watford post, which had been vacated by Dave Bassett. Taylor filled Harrison's job with another former contact, John Ward, who had played under him at Lincoln City and latterly working at Watford, where he had been Taylor's assistant.

Taylor soon took his revenge on Harrison for leaving by snatching the signature of the exciting

Crewe Alexandra midfielder David Platt for £200,000. Platt was set for a move to Vicarage Road until Taylor sniffed the deal. He subsequently scored a goal in each of his first three matches for Villa and played a vital role in the promotion push from February 1988.

Villa were promoted back to the First Division after just a single year in the second tier, bouncing back from a gradual decline since the heights of being European champions in 1982. A lack of investment in the transfer market and the constant sales of their best player assets eventually took its toll. Until, that is, Taylor set about the rebuilding work.

Ellis rarely satisfied the Villa supporters, but the fans would have to acknowledge Ellis got it right with the appointment. He arrived with a reputation as a manager who liked to play the 'long ball' at Vicarage Road. But in fairness to him and his coaches, his brand at Villa might have been direct with tall strikers such as Alan McInally, Garry Thompson and the rookie Ian Olney, but the football was usually vibrant and exciting.

One of the first moves that Taylor made on winning promotion was to convince Ellis to bring the popular legend Gordon Cowans back from Italian club

Bari, as Villa still held 'first option' on his signature. It was another shrewd move.

Taylor was not only a master of the transfer market and handling Ellis – he also knew the importance of team spirit, which was one of the reasons why a mediocre team like Watford that often relied on the brilliance of John Barnes and the goals of Luther Blissett was able to believe in themselves enough to finish second in the top flight in the 1982/83 season, and reach the FA Cup Final a year later.

The boss once took Villa on a team bonding trip to a Pontins holiday camp, when he'd allowed the players to think they were going somewhere more exotic after telling them to bring their passports. Still, the end goal was achieved when a healthy team spirit had been garnered prior to their return to the First Division. Perhaps the most comical moment of the trip came once he found out where Steve Sims had been going when he was supposed to be with the team. Sims, supposedly injured, had entered himself in a bowls competition against dozens of elderly holidaymakers.

Once Taylor found out, there was no rant or disciplinary action. Instead, he ensured the rest of the squad were present to cheer on Sims in his semi-final clash. That was vintage Taylor. Not only did he make his point that he would always find out if players were being sneaky behind his back, but he did it by still managing to create a fun environment with the rest of the squad.

On another occasion, the team embarked on a more exciting trip than the English coastline, to Spain. On such trips, managers were always slightly concerned the players would misbehave once they were allowed the freedom of so many bars and the luxury of alcohol.

'After we got promoted, Doug paid for all the players to go to Marbella for a week,' Garry Thompson said. 'We were drinking, carrying on and having fun as you do. But Platty was a bit distant. When Platty first came to the club, myself, Gary Shaw, McInally and Andy Gray would take him out for something to eat so he wasn't sitting in a hotel on his own and was spending time getting to know the lads.

'Anyway, in Marbella, me and Shawry had a word with him after a few drinks and said, "What's the matter with you, you're acting all quiet and strange." Platty then explained that the gaffer had advised him to stay away from some of the lads, "especially Shaw and Thompson because all they want to do is get pissed and chase birds". I don't blame Platty for that, he was doing what he thought he had to do.'

Inevitably, Taylor added to his promotion winners with more quality to help Villa through that first campaign back in the top flight. Derek Mountfield was signed from Everton for £400,000 in June 1988. The centre-half, born and bred in the Wirral, brought good pedigree with him having won two English league titles, an FA Cup and a Cup Winners' Cup. He had formed a reliable central defensive partnership with Kevin Ratcliffe at Goodison Park but found himself surplus to requirements once the Toffees recruited Dave Watson from Norwich City. Taylor was quick to spot a player who he thought could help take Villa to the next level.

'I'd had a difficult couple of years at Everton, partly because of a knee injury and partly because of Dave coming in,' Mountfield said. 'I no longer felt a part of the team and mentioned to the manager Colin Harvey that I didn't want to go on the pre-season tour to Magaluf [in 1988]. I didn't expect to leave Everton that summer because I still had a year left on my contract, but things changed very quickly.

'The next thing, Villa had been in touch and both clubs had agreed a fee. I met with Graham Taylor and it soon became clear that moving to Aston Villa would be a great move for me. It gave me my appetite back for football. At Everton, I had gone from someone who was a first-team regular and winning trophies to being on the fringes, sitting in the stands watching the first team and playing reserve team games. Graham gave me my spark back.'

Mountfield was virtually a household name in English football at that stage given the medals he had accrued. But Taylor was not a manager who only liked to recruit established talent. He was prepared to take a punt on someone if he believed he had something he could work with and nurture.

Bradford City attacker Ian Ormondroyd would be one of the more extreme examples. Taylor invested £650,000 on the 6ft 5in Yorkshireman and signed him in February 1989, along with right-winger from Derby County Nigel Callaghan, who he had worked with at Watford. Few Villa supporters would have remembered that Ormondroyd had scored for Bradford in a shock 5-0 win at Villa Park the season before in the Full Members' Cup.

'That was a strange result,' recalled Ormondroyd with a chuckle. 'Then Villa pipped us by a point in the league to go up ahead of us.

'I was a hometown boy and it was a bit of a shock when Villa came calling. But I was going from a middling team in the old Second Division to a massive club that had an incredible history. I knew I had to go to try and improve myself, but it was a big jump for me. The huge transfer fee was an added burden because the expectancy levels were high.'

Ormondroyd, warmly nicknamed 'Sticks' by the Villa fans for his beanpole frame and long, skinny legs, was able to help his new club to a 2-0 win on debut at home to Sheffield Wednesday. Soon, his wife would be able to watch most of his home matches from the Holte End as she transferred from West Yorkshire Police to the West Midlands and often worked on matchdays as an officer in charge of crowd control. Future manager Ron Atkinson mischievously retold a quip by team physio Jim Walker. It is said that Mrs Ormondroyd was heard in the players' lounge after a match complaining about the level of abuse that her Ian was receiving, and she was tempted to arrest them. 'In that case,' Walker interjected, 'you'd have arrested the whole of the bloody Holte End!'

Villa endured a difficult season back in the First Division, finishing on 40 points and one place above the relegation zone in 17th and just a single point ahead of relegated Middlesbrough, who went down with bottom club Newcastle and West Ham. Villa won only two of their last 15 league games and managed a 1-1 draw in their last game of the season at home to local rivals Coventry City. Atkinson's Sheffield Wednesday beat Boro 1-0 and helped themselves and Villa to steer clear of the drop. Interestingly, the Owls were relegated a year later, with 43 points!

The campaign had started encouragingly enough with no defeats in their first six matches and a 3-2 win against Arsenal away at Highbury in the second league game. McInally notched two of those goals and he eventually scored 22 for the season, despite the team's indifferent results.

His haul included two against Millwall in the third round of the League Cup, the second being one of the goals of the season. He collected a punch from goalkeeper Nigel Spink midway in his own half before beating three Millwall players and slipping the ball past opposition keeper Brian Horne.

'It was a season of transition,' reflected Gage, who missed the last two months after getting badly injured at Millwall. Kevin O'Callaghan's tackle injured his knee ligaments and kept him out for six months.

'That was the season where I started playing in midfield. Initially, Chris Price was brought in to compete with me for the right-back position and, somehow, he got the nod over me, which I wasn't too pleased about as I had been an ever-present in the promotion year. But Graham knew where he was taking this squad, and he knew I could play in midfield. It worked out well until I got injured.'

Taylor phoned all the players at the end of what was a difficult campaign, with an important message. This was where his sublime man-management skills came to the fore. In one sense, he was praising them for avoiding a second relegation in three seasons. But more poignantly, he was already setting about raising the bar and he needed his players to respond accordingly.

'Graham kept saying, that first season back was all about survival,' winger Tony Daley revealed. 'But what stuck in my mind was when he called me at my home as soon as our survival was assured. He said, "Well done this season, staying up is a great success. But next season we are going to kick on. We are going to go places." He actually said those words. He filled me with confidence – it was nice to hear. But I honestly never expected to do as well as we did the following year.'

1988/89 season:

League position: 17th (of 20)

League Cup: quarter-final (lost 2-1 at West Ham United)

FA Cup: fourth round (lost 1-0 at home to Wimbledon)

Full Members' Cup: second round (lost 2-1 at Derby County)

Top scorers: Alan McInally 22; David Platt 15; Kevin Gage 7

2

Villa in Limbo? After Losing Rambo

'People thought once McInally left, we were going to struggle but we simply didn't miss him.'

– Derek Mountfield

ALLAN EVANS' 12-year Aston Villa career came to a natural end in the summer of 1989 as Graham Taylor set about plans for a more ambitious season in the top flight. But in truth there were only two transfers which resonated with the Villa supporters at that time: one incoming, one outgoing.

The sale of Holte End hero Alan McInally for £1.3m to Bayern Munich was a hammer blow to the fans who had taken him to their hearts. 'Spinksy and Birchy, Alan McInally …' Incredibly, those words bellowed from the terraces have stood the test of time in subsequent decades, which is some compliment to a striker who spent just two years at Villa. His rampaging runs, his commitment and, especially, his goals struck a chord with the fans.

It was reluctantly accepted when he left for Germany, as supporters were realistic enough to know McInally was unlikely to reject a move to Bayern Munich and the subsequent European matches that came with it, which English clubs then could not offer. And besides, Villa had proven consistently over the years they were a club willing to sell their best players for the right price.

The difference here, though, is not well known. McInally has revealed more than 30 years later that he offered to snub the move away from Villa if the club was prepared to improve his contract. Typically, Doug Ellis opted to take the £1m profit on a player he paid £225,000 for from Celtic.

'It was a difficult one as I was happy at Aston Villa,' McInally recalled. 'I still had two years of my contract left to run and I was never leaving the club. That's how I felt.

'It wasn't until Bayern came in that Graham indicated there was interest in me. He felt obligated to tell me they had been watching me play for Scotland

and Aston Villa. It all happened very quickly. He knew I might never have that opportunity again in my career.

'I was still in no rush to leave, though, and I said to Graham, "Give me a new, improved contract and I'll stay." If they had done that, I would definitely have stayed. My daughter was born at Good Hope Hospital in Sutton Coldfield, she was about three then, I was loving life at Villa and where I was based in Lichfield.

'Mr Ellis looked after me really well at Villa, but he wasn't prepared to give me a new contract in light of the Bayern interest. It became clear then I wasn't going to get a new contract and that Bayern were not taking no for an answer, as they needed a centre-forward. I had an unofficial pact with Graham that I wouldn't go to another English club, so this was OK with him.

'Only two players left to go to a European club the year I went. Me and Chris Waddle, who went to Marseille. They were both great moves for our careers but there's always some sadness when you leave a club you're happy at.

'OK, I was suddenly rubbing shoulders with greats of the game like Uli Hoeneß, Gerd Müller, Franz Beckenbauer and Karl-Heinz Rummenigge, which was surreal. But I really loved Villa and I left before I achieved what I wanted to.

'Even after leaving I still used to speak to Stuart Gray and David Platt to find out what was going on at Villa, "How did the game go last weekend, etc?"'

Villa's then secretary Steve Stride remembered that Taylor considered the move a good deal for the club and an opportunity that McInally should not give up. Unlike some football managers who can be ruthless in favour of their own aspirations, Taylor was one who looked at the player's viewpoint. He recognised Bayern Munich as a significant and successful club in global terms and was not going to stand in McInally's way.

The departure of McInally initially caused a ripple of discontent in the dressing room, as often happens at the sale of a club's talisman. The thought, 'Who's going to score Macca's goals now?' was speculated on. But as ever, the game goes on and the club will always prove greater than any individual. Just like when Ron Saunders sold two of his best players in 1979: the exits of Andy Gray and John Gidman left supporters devastated. A third would also have left had Brian Little not failed a fitness test at Birmingham City. Despite the initial gloom, unexpected and unprecedented success followed soon after.

'You're not happy and are a bit perturbed when one of your best players goes,' Kevin Gage said. 'But other players come in and life goes on. Villa had the resources to go out and replace him and young Ian Olney came in, also.'

Captain Stuart Gray acknowledged it was an unbelievable move for McInally who, as one of the early British players to be exported to Europe, couldn't really say no. Gray reflected philosophically and suggested the team never missed him as much as they might have expected because David Platt developed rapidly and started to score goals prolifically.

'McInally was very strong and Graham made sure we played to his strengths,' Gray said. 'We never played balls into his feet, they'd be over the top for him to run on to or in the channels, out wide. Things clicked for him and he scored all types of goals. There is no doubt he was a key man for us up front and would take some replacing. Not only that, but it would mean we needed a change of style.'

One of McInally's closest friends at Villa was his fellow striker, Garry Thompson. He also felt it was a transfer the Scottish goalscorer could not turn down, 'He tore it up to earn his move to Bayern, he was a different class, and fair play to him. I think, though, if he's honest he would admit to feeling like he left Villa before he really wanted to. He's a legend at Villa and only had two seasons there, but obviously, he couldn't turn that move down. Nobody in their right mind would have denied him that.

'We used to have a bath together after a game and talk about all kinds of shit and one day he said, "I've got to tell you something; I need to tell someone. I've been having conversations with Bayern Munich. I'm going to be out of here." I said, "Fuck off!" Then he said, "No, it's pretty much done and dusted, Doug has agreed it."

'I loved the big fella, but I still didn't believe him. But soon I was off to Watford and, later, he was off to Germany!'

Defender Derek Mountfield was equally in awe of McInally's contribution to Villa and wasn't happy about his exit from Villa Park. However, the former Everton man felt, in hindsight, that losing McInally was something of a blessing in disguise because it made the team stronger as a group and players contributed goals from all over the park when, previously, there seemed to be a reliance on McInally to deliver.

'He was a very good player and a larger-than-life character in the dressing room and he still is a great character now,' Mountfield said. 'People thought once Macca left, we were going to struggle but we simply didn't miss him. When a team loses its best player, the obvious conclusion is that the team will struggle without him, but it doesn't always work out like that, and instead other players come to the fore.

'Macca scored a lot of goals for us but very few other players scored. Once he left, we got goals from other parts of the pitch like David Platt especially, Ian Ormondroyd, Tony Daley and Ian Olney did a fantastic job to replace him. We came together as a team and made it work and people would have been surprised by how well we did without having Macca around. And he went on to have a fantastic career himself with Bayern Munich and beyond, so everything worked out.'

Ian Olney made his Villa debut in the survival season of 1988/89, scoring in his first match, against bitter rivals Birmingham City in a 5-0 League Cup second round demolition. He went on to make 18 first-team appearances as Taylor identified enough potential to allow him more opportunities post-McInally. In fact, he rated the six-footer so well as a striker able to hold the ball up and bring others into play that he did not immediately replace McInally and instead placed his faith in the youngster.

'People forget about Ian Olney,' Gage reflected. 'He came in from the reserves after we sold McInally for a lot of money and he had big boots to fill, but he did really well. He was brilliant up front, holding the ball up.'

Thompson added on Olney, 'I played in the reserves with him a few times. He always looked a bit gangly, but he had a goal in him. He put himself around and really stepped up to the plate once Macca left.'

The presence of Olney persuaded Taylor to use his £650,000 signing Ian Ormondroyd in a different way than he had first envisaged. He was supposed to be the tall, aerially combative ball-winning target man that George Reilly had been for him at Watford. But Taylor threw that plan out and created something fresh that worked like a charm.

'When Graham signed me, I think the plan was to play me at centre-forward,' Ormondroyd said. 'But the more he saw me in training he felt I was better facing the opposition goal rather than having my back to their goal like an Ian Olney. I was OK in the air but for my size I wasn't brilliant at heading. So that also influenced his thinking in moving me out to the left wing.

'It turned out to be a bit of a master stroke from him because I ended up playing the rest of my career on the left of midfield or on the left of a front three. Only Arthur Cox at Derby played me as a centre-forward, as he was more of an old-fashioned 4-4-2-type coach.

'I was never going to be a Tony Daley-type winger doing step-overs and skinning the full-back. But I could beat a man and get a good cross in. The aerial threat I posed out wide was useful for us, because most right-backs I played against were small and were not used to playing against such a tall winger.

'So many right-backs didn't know what to do, so managers ended up swapping the centre-half over with the right-back, and the plan just disrupted opposition plans against us. It worked a treat.'

Gage agreed that Taylor's thinking regarding Ormondroyd was something of a magical recipe that gave Villa a unique asset going forward.

'He was one of the most ungainly footballers you will ever see but was hugely effective,' said Gage. 'He wasn't blessed with the greatest ability but was decent enough on the ball. We used to play him out on the left wing and he used to whip in some great crosses, which often led to goals.'

So, with key striker McInally gone, club veteran Evans gone, and with defensive prodigy Martin Keown opting to leave what he thought was a sinking ship for the prosperity of Everton, it was a time of further change at Villa Park. Incidentally, Keown said he would never have left if he had known the identity of the new central defender that Taylor was bringing in.

If supporters began to feel any negativity at the transfer situation looking ahead to the 1989/90 campaign, the mood lifted when an established Republic of Ireland defender signed in August 1989 from Manchester United.

Paul McGrath, then just 29, was simply unwanted at United. Alex Ferguson attempted to disrupt the drinking culture within the team, which McGrath had been part of, along with Bryan Robson, Norman Whiteside and others. England's 'Captain Marvel' Robson was never going to be sold, but Whiteside left for Everton weeks before McGrath's exit.

Ferguson also deemed both players injury-prone and was of the opinion McGrath's dodgy knees were ready to give out.

Therefore, the £400,000 that Aston Villa paid for him was a gamble, but one that was well worth taking according to Graham Taylor. How right he would later prove to be.

3

God!

'We all know Paul never trained in the week but once he put a kit on, come game day he then showed why he was rightly known as God.'

– Derek Mountfield

PAUL MCGRATH was one of the toughest and best defenders of his generation, having endured one of the roughest, most difficult upbringings a wannabe footballer could possibly have, with a lack of typical family life behind him. Yet, despite this background, he was frightened to death of leaving Manchester United.

At Old Trafford, since arriving in 1983 from Irish club St Patrick's, he had been settled in Manchester, often cocooned with his regular drinking mates. His fallouts with the volatile manager Alex Ferguson had worsened, but the club and city *was* his home, his everything. If he was ever going to leave, he wanted it to be to Tottenham Hotspur.

Eventually, by the summer of 1989, McGrath knew his time at United under Ferguson's strict regime was over. United encouraged him to retire so that they could claim off the insurance policy. There was a chance the stubborn Ferguson was making a huge mistake by trying to retire him, but he was never one to be proved wrong. McGrath, though, was not interested in retirement.

Ron Atkinson, the manager who took McGrath to United and the boss when he won an FA Cup winners' medal in 1985, offered United £150,000 for the Irishman when he was in charge at Sheffield Wednesday. That cheeky bid, though, was destined to fail once Aston Villa made it known they were prepared to pay the £425,000 that Fergie was asking for.

McGrath and his wife Claire met Graham Taylor, Doug Ellis and secretary Steve Stride on a Sunday afternoon, in an effort to avoid unwanted publicity, with the intention of signing for Villa. Typically, according to Taylor, Claire did all the talking as McGrath was naturally shy. A warm, mutually respectful relationship began to form between the manager and his new star player.

Villa almost tripled McGrath's salary, as Taylor broke the club's tight wage structure to sign him. Who said Doug Ellis and Villa were tight? McGrath started on a little more than £3,000 a week.

He was to be unveiled to the media the following day along with Denmark international Kent Nielsen, who joined from Danish side Brondby for £500,000. Once McGrath knew he was to be the centre of attention in a press conference that was pretty much all about him, with respect to the lesser-known Nielsen, the defender panicked.

Taylor picked up the players from their West Bromwich hotel and McGrath sat in the back talking non-stop, which was a total opposite to the person he was starting to get to know. Taylor asked him later if he had been drinking on the press conference day and McGrath admitted he had consumed a bottle of Southern Comfort to calm his nerves.

'Paul hated that sort of thing because he was such a shy person,' Stride commented. 'He hated being the focal point in a room. Paul turned up on the Monday and I took one look at him and could tell that his eyes were glazed. He was obviously pissed. He wasn't falling over or slurring his words, but he wasn't as he should be. I knew that was his way of trying to make himself calm for that press conference. He said to me, "I'd rather not do it," but I said, "You've got to do it, Paul." So reluctantly he did it with no problems.'

Not everyone was so pleased about McGrath's arrival. Derek Mountfield had seen three of his former central defensive partners depart over the summer, yet once he became aware of the capture of McGrath, and Kent Nielsen too, he knew the pressure was on him if he still wanted to prove a point to those who felt Everton were justified in offloading him to Villa.

'I thought I needed to buck my ideas up as here was someone trying to take my place,' Mountfield admitted. 'Sometimes you need someone to put pressure on you. And when Kent Nielsen came in with Macca, I did wonder about my place. The season before there was me, Steve Sims, Allan Evans and Martin Keown but three of those guys left in that 1989 summer so it was at least encouraging that I was still there.

'In the event, it was a privilege to play alongside Paul. We all know he never trained in the week but once he put a kit on, come game day he then showed why he was rightly known as God. He would have to be one of the best players in Villa's history because he was truly magnificent in every game he played pretty much.'

Taylor deserved much credit for the way he never concerned himself too much with what McGrath did in training, or didn't do more to the point, if he was ready on matchdays. And by some miracle, he usually was.

Managers generally know which players they need to show the stick to, and which ones need the proverbial carrot, or maybe an arm around the shoulder in real terms. Players have always accepted this over the years in the knowledge that everyone is different and not one message or approach suits all. The only thing that players really expect off managers is honesty and fairness and that they all operate under the same rulebook. In the case of McGrath, Taylor was clever enough to know he had to offer him special treatment to reap the performances from him that he hoped for.

'Graham Taylor worked us hard in pre-season, real hard,' Villa midfield legend Gordon Cowans recalled. 'In one of the first sessions, he made us do six laps around the training ground. Paul just tagged on at the back. He couldn't do it. And from that moment on, he just seemed to go to the gym and do his own thing.

'The lads didn't care, because they quickly saw how good he was and how important he became to the team. Normally in that situation, there might be an attitude of, "This fella's taking the piss …" But Paul wasn't taking the piss. He genuinely had a problem with his knee. We all knew that. But he was such a wonderful player, we needed him in the team on a Saturday.'

The different training regime was one thing, to accommodate McGrath's fragile knees, but that wasn't the only special dispensation they all knew was being afforded him. His drinking habit was unofficially accepted as a disease within the club; the alcoholism had to be managed on a day-to-day basis. The true star in this regard was club physio Jim Walker.

McGrath revealed in his autobiography that Walker was so dedicated towards him that his loyalty could have cost him his job at times, such was the extent that he covered for him.

Interestingly, McGrath had eight knee operations at United and not even one at Villa because of the way they managed him. Where his team-mates might have been doing ball skills or heavy fitness work, McGrath was peacefully riding the exercise bike in the gym, supervised by Walker.

'Jim was excellent and was quick to realise that the club's assets are out on the pitch, so nobody wanted them in the treatment room,' Stuart Gray commented. 'Maybe the modern physios feel they aren't doing their job unless their treatment room has a few players in, but Jim wasn't bothered about that. He was a unique physio because he had a great understanding of the game and contributed in lots of ways to the team cause.'

Kevin Richardson, McGrath's future captain under the Ron Atkinson regime, never felt that he needed to chide or speak directly to the Irishman about his off-field escapades because it was commonly accepted by the players that he was a special case, who had certain challenges, yet they somehow did not affect performance.

'It was a case of just let him be,' Richardson said. 'When he did something good, tell him. When he did something wrong on the pitch I didn't have to tell him, nobody did, because he knew it himself. It wasn't very often.

'But to this day I don't know how he managed to play as well as he did so often. A fantastic player. Imagine what he could have been and the levels he could have reached without the problems that he had in his personal life? The best clubs in Europe must have been interested in him if he wasn't as troubled in his private life as he was.

'The way he never trained and then would be man of the match week in and week out, I just don't know how he did it.'

McGrath was aware of the saying about any footballer who leaves Manchester United is only destined for a downhill journey thereafter. But he felt his move to Villa did the opposite.

It made him. A legend reborn. The birth of God.

4

Old Foe Haunts the Villa

'Five minutes from the end, Paul [McGrath] fell down in the penalty box. I whispered to Jim Walker, "Go and tell him that all I want him to do is stand up."'

– Graham Taylor

ANY EARLY season optimism soon transformed to scepticism. Early results did not reassure supporters this campaign would be any better than the last. It was, after all, meant to be a season of progression.

Fans were already in despair over the sales of the previous season's top scorer, Alan McInally, and England hopeful Martin Keown. They were desperate to see signs of encouragement, somewhere. The £300,000 signing of Adrian Heath from Espanyol was unlikely to provide the kind of hope they were looking for given his best was mostly behind him at Stoke City and Everton.

An opening day 1-1 draw at Brian Clough's Nottingham Forest was pleasing enough after Derek Mountfield's early goal was cancelled out in the second half. Taylor employed a three-man central defence with Mountfield alongside debutants Kent Nielsen and Paul McGrath. The plan was for McGrath to sit and mop up the loose balls that the other two warriors challenged for.

Another 1-1 draw at Villa Park was hard-earned against Liverpool's team of legends managed by Kenny Dalglish. John Barnes, Peter Beardsley, Ian Rush, Alan Hansen et al couldn't find a way to beat Taylor's men so there were seeds of promise in terms of their resilience. David Platt opened his account for the season, in which he eventually notched 24 goals in all competitions. But at this stage there was little evidence he would replace McInally's goal count.

A third straight 1-1 draw at home to Charlton Athletic and a 2-1 defeat at Southampton put Villa in 15th. A brilliant 2-0 home win against Tottenham, including Paul Gascoigne and Gary Lineker, was then tempered by another disappointing result, losing 1-0 at Sheffield Wednesday – managed by Ron Atkinson and with his namesake Dalian scoring the goal.

The worst was to come, though, as Queens Park Rangers visited Villa Park under the leadership of player-manager Trevor Francis. The classy striker had been a constant thorn in Villa's side for Birmingham City in local derbies in the 1970s. He was despised by Villa supporters only because they feared him, even respected him.

But surely now, in September 1989 and almost 14 years to the day since he scored his first goal against Villa, surely, he would no longer pose the same threat? He was 35 after all, and a decade had passed since his diving header gave Nottingham Forest an unlikely European Cup Final victory against Malmö.

Wrong. He scored a hat-trick to give QPR a spectacular 3-1 win after Platt had put Villa ahead early on. QPR included several players in their ranks who many would have considered past their best such as Kenny Sansom, Peter Reid, Nigel Spackman and Francis, but there were also future England stars David Seaman, Paul Parker and Andy Sinton, and Northern Ireland veterans Alan McDonald and Colin Clarke. The defeat meant Villa plummeted to 17th. The goals were a painful reminder of the Francis magic of old.

For the first, Nigel Spink failed to hold on to a cross-shot from the right and the loose ball was fired home first time by Francis from 18 yards out.

The second came as a corner from the right was flicked on at the near post and Francis rose above Kevin Gage to head home from close range.

To complete his hat-trick, Francis controlled a headed clearance and before the ball bounced, he volleyed a right-footed shot into the top corner of Spink's goal – it went in off the underside of the bar from 20 yards out, proving he still had magic in his boots.

'I played with Trevor at Nottingham Forest, we even shared the same birthday, so I was aware of the threat he posed as a goalscorer though he was obviously past his heyday by this game,' Stuart Gray said. 'Old habits die hard, though, and the old Villa–Blues rivalry just added a bit of spice to this game of course as nobody has ever seen a more bitter rivalry than the Villa–Birmingham City one. It was a painful day for us as a team and for the fans. But Graham didn't seem to panic and just got back on to the training ground to try to sort things out.'

The low attendance of just 14,170 proved how supporters were turned off by the poor start to the season.

'We played poorly in that match,' Derek Mountfield acknowledged. 'After Trevor scored that lob for his hat-trick, I remember thinking to myself, "Gordon Bennett, he's a player and a half." It was one of those games. We had some at Everton when we won the league, games you should win but they go against you for some reason. I think it's important that you react in the right way to results like that and fortunately, we reacted well to that QPR game.'

Behind the scenes, matters were critical. Tactics were not working. Players were playing below par and Graham Taylor was becoming increasingly concerned by McGrath's off-field drinking, and now believed he was bringing this issue to matchdays, too.

'Five minutes from the end [of the QPR match], Paul fell down in the penalty box,' Taylor remembered. 'I whispered to Jim Walker, "Go and tell him that all I want him to do is stand up."

'I could see then I had a big problem. We had won one of our first seven league games and I was in a bit of trouble. I remember going into the dressing room after and looking at Paul. He wouldn't look at me. I had heard that he liked a drink, but I hadn't actually realised I had taken on an alcoholic. I was very, very disturbed.'

The following game against Derby County at home was won 1-0 but Villa and McGrath were not much better than they had been against QPR. They benefitted from some missed chances, uncharacteristically, by Rams striker Dean Saunders.

What supporters were not aware of then was that on the morning of the Derby match, Taylor considered handing in his resignation. Things had become that bad.

'It was a Saturday morning,' Steve Stride said, 'on the day we played Derby County and Graham came in to see me and asked if the chairman was in. I told him he wasn't in yet. This would be at about midday. He confided to me that he was thinking of giving in his notice before Doug sacked him, as we hadn't got off to the best of starts that season.

'The chairman's reputation for sacking managers was such that Graham was genuinely worried he was going to get the bullet. I like to think I talked him out of it. I said, "Don't be silly, Graham. I'll tell you now the chairman is not thinking of sacking you. Because if he was, I'd know about it."

'There was never any talk of Doug sacking him and I don't even remember Doug having doubts about

Graham. If that poor run had carried on, maybe. But it never did. Graham said, "OK, I'll give it some more thought after the game." Somehow, we managed to beat Derby and it was the turning point in that season and the rest is history.'

Stuart Gray did not detect any difference in Taylor, despite his obvious disappointment at the run of poor results.

'I didn't see any difference in Graham, but ultimately the expectation of the Villa fans when you're playing at home is to win so the QPR game would have hurt him and disappointed the fans,' Gray said. 'Sometimes you have to win ugly to keep your job and fortunately for Graham we managed to do that in the next game against Derby. These things are all part of being a manager.'

Equally, Tony Daley was also oblivious to Taylor's off-field anguish and was relieved in hindsight that the team was able to put an end to their nightmare run of results.

'I didn't know that Graham was considering handing in his resignation but there were certainly rumours in the media that if we lost to Derby he would get the sack,' Daley recalled. 'We were shocking in that match. Dean Saunders missed a couple of chances, but Platty scored a vital goal, and it turned out to be a trigger point to spark us off.

'We went on an unbelievable run after that game. I was pleased because I enjoyed playing under Graham. He was so good for my career, on and off the field. I don't think professional footballers ever want a manager to get the sack even if they don't like them. But, subconsciously, when a team is really behind a manager you do strain that bit more to block shots, run that bit more to track back, and try harder to do as well as you can for the manager and the team.'

Paul McGrath was always very honest about his own contribution to the team and was aware that he had not started his Aston Villa career in the way he would have wanted.

'Those games with QPR and Derby were horrendous,' McGrath later admitted. 'Trevor Francis was effectively at the end of his career. He was QPR's oldest player. The goals he got against me were ridiculous. I remember thinking to myself, "This can't be happening." Villa must have been wondering what on earth they had brought upon themselves … It wasn't that I was actually drinking before the game. I wasn't. But I was certainly drinking too much generally. My head was all over the place.'

If Taylor, Stride and McGrath thought their problems were behind them after the relief of a rare victory over Derby, they were hugely mistaken. Their stresses were only just starting.

Between the Derby County match and the next game at Luton Town (dismissing a League Cup tie with Wolves), McGrath suffered a serious breakdown which culminated with him purposely cutting his wrists with a knife in front of his toddler son.

Emergency services were called, and Jim Walker and Graham Taylor were wondering what to do next. McGrath checked into the Priory Hospital in Edgbaston, Birmingham, under a different name to avoid unwanted publicity – even his team-mates did not know. The issues in McGrath's private life meant he was out of the team for a month.

This was the turning point and when McGrath the injury-prone drunk slowly transformed into what Villa fans forever knew him as, God. McGrath would come into the training ground for treatment on a hamstring injury, or at least that was the cover story.

Before returning to his temporary home at the Priory, he would go into Taylor's office and open up on his inner demons, which was not something that came easy for him. This was the time when Taylor realised there was more to McGrath's problems than drink and a lack of professionalism. It was also the time when McGrath started to put total trust in Taylor and revealed all on what he had been through in his life. McGrath was famously shy and quiet, not a big talker, but he felt he had already let Taylor and Villa down by the start he had made at the club. Therefore, he needed to explain himself.

'He started opening up to me, about his background, about his breakdown,' Taylor revealed. 'And I'm sat there thinking, "Oh my goodness …"

'It was as if he needed to get all this off his chest. I remember going home a couple of evenings after those chats. I shared a lot of things with my wife. I'd talk a lot of things through with her. And I remember saying to her one evening, "Tell you what, it's all right saying to someone they shouldn't be doing this or shouldn't be doing that, but I think I'd be drinking too if I'd been through what Paul's been through." Listening to him, it was actually hard not to cry.'

Once McGrath had bared his soul to Taylor and accepted his issues and was prepared to deal with them, they developed a bond that was unusually personal and strong between a player and manager.

It was no coincidence that McGrath's performances improved dramatically thereafter.

McGrath said, 'I had liked Graham Taylor from the first time we spoke ... the thing that struck me above all else was that he was interested in me. He had every reason to be furious. One of his big summer signings had turned out to be a walking mess. I couldn't have argued if he was obnoxious and turned on me saying, "What the fuck are you like, you dozy twat?" But he was open and caring. I always felt welcome in his office ... I felt I could talk to him on a level I had probably never talked on with anyone in football.

'I don't think I'm being melodramatic when I say he literally rescued me from a bad, bad scene.

'Under another manager, I suspect my career might have been over. But Graham Taylor's sensitivity worked wonders. The more we talked, the more determined I became to repay him. I felt this urge inside, I wanted to play for this man, to win things.'

McGrath's problems were treated with the utmost discretion. His team-mates never knew the extent of what he had gone through. His medical records had to be handled carefully so it was only Jim Walker and the club doctor who knew.

Secrets remained secret until McGrath released his autobiography in 2006.

That compassionate kid-gloves approach by Taylor was rewarded by McGrath going on to enjoy what were probably the best days of his career, subsequently. His outstanding performances at the 1990 and 1994 World Cups for the Republic of Ireland placed him at least on a par with the best centre-halves in the world.

Curiously, McGrath's problems coincided with a five-match winning run in the league and he played in the fifth of them, a 6-2 thrashing of Everton. He scored a late own goal, but he was otherwise impeccable playing in a deep midfield role, sweeping in front of the defence and stopping his old drinking partner Norman Whiteside from causing any damage, creatively. Villa didn't lose another game in the league for almost six weeks, when they were beaten at Norwich City.

From the Everton match onwards, McGrath never missed another match, playing 35 games in 38. He was even voted the supporters' player of the year.

Mountfield said, 'We knew Paul was having problems, with the alcohol, with his knees and everything else. But Graham and the club were very good in keeping his issues away from the rest of the team, and from the media.

'Graham and Jim Walker managed him exceptionally to keep him on the park and to keep his career going. I used to drive Paul down from Manchester when he was first at Villa, but he was a closed book. He would come into training, do his thing, and then go back to his digs. He wasn't a loner, but he had his own routine and we all respected that.

'What a footballer and what a person as well. As a footballer he's up there with any player who has ever played the game, certainly from Ireland. He must be up there with the top three players who ever wore the Villa shirt.'

5

Villa Toast Toffees on Bonfire Night, and the Rise of Platt

'With every win we started to gain in confidence, especially after that Everton result. We went to Chelsea on New Year's Day and won 3-0 on the back of home wins against Manchester United and Arsenal. By that time a lot of the players started to think we could win the league.'

– Kevin Gage

GOALS FROM Ian Ormondroyd and David Platt helped Villa dismantle a star-studded Tottenham Hotspur on 21 February. It was a significant result on several levels, but more than anything, the 2-0 win projected them to the summit of the First Division.

It was Villa's seventh consecutive victory as they rose above Liverpool to the top of the table. They made light work of Terry Venables' Spurs team inclusive of England players Gary Lineker, Paul Gascoigne, Paul Walsh and defensive kingpin Gary Mabbutt.

'My confidence and the team's confidence was growing all the time, we were flying,' winger Tony Daley reflected. 'We went to Tottenham and beat them with ease. We could not do any wrong.

'I was going out on to the field thinking, "I'm going to be a nightmare for their full-back today, Platty's going to score, they'll never get through our defence." I just had so much belief in myself and the team that I thought it was going to take us all the way. We weren't arrogant, we were just brimming with so much confidence.'

Ormondroyd added, 'I enjoyed scoring at Tottenham in that win. They told Pat Van Den Hauwe to mark me and all he did all game was kick me up in the air, so it was very satisfying to win that match. It showed once again that we were good enough to beat the top teams.'

While that Tottenham result was significant, it was the 6-2 demolition of Everton – who were English champions two years prior – that really sparked genuine belief among the team that Villa just might be capable of achieving something to be proud of that season. It was the result, according to Kevin Gage, that made the whole country sit up and take notice of Villa.

On Bonfire Night and in front of a rare live television audience, the players chose their moment perfectly to announce themselves as a team worthy of upsetting the league's hierarchies, if not outright title contenders. Ormondroyd believed it was like a coming together of several journeymen like himself, Gage, Chris Price, Ian Olney and more with the sheer quality of players like Paul McGrath, David Platt and Gordon Cowans.

Cowans, Olney (two), Platt (two) and Kent Nielsen put Villa 6-0 up by the 67th minute. Two late goals courtesy of a McGrath own goal and Tony Cottee in the 83rd and 85th minutes slightly reduced the humiliation for Everton.

Stuart Gray remembered that Adrian Heath was fuming that he wasn't playing against his old club, though he went on as sub later in the game when Villa were 6-0 up.

'Adrian threw his boots on the dressing room floor after the match as he badly wanted to play against his old club,' Gray said. 'Jim Walker, who had a great dry sense of humour, said it was a good job he didn't play longer as we might have drew!'

Derek Mountfield was another ex-Toffees man, and he also felt some annoyance at the end of the match, but for a different reason.

'We felt disappointed to let those two late goals in,' Mountfield remembered. 'We were so comfortable that we thought we should have won 7-, 8- or 9-0. We tore them apart that day.

'It was one of the most satisfying games of my career. After I left Everton, not quite under a cloud, some people were suggesting I was finished, and my career would go down from there. So that performance gave me an awful lot of pleasure.

'We went to Kevin Gage's house afterwards for a bonfire party. It was lovely and even better after a result like that!'

Ormondroyd was one of the key ingredients to Everton's downfall that day as they struggled to deal with his height and unorthodox wing work on the left flank.

'I remember that game fondly,' Ormondroyd said, 'not just because of the result but because Nigel Spink kept drop-kicking his goal kicks straight on my head and they put Stuart McCall to right-back to try to stop the tactic, but he couldn't because I was obviously a lot taller than him. I played at Bradford City with

Stuart and he was a good midfielder but, in that game, he had a tough gig.'

It was their fifth straight win and was the game that McGrath returned from his personal problems. The return to a three-man central defence with Nielsen and Mountfield was another key development that served Villa well for the remainder of the season. It was a precursor to how Bobby Robson's switch to three at the back a few months later at Italia '90 changed England's fortunes too.

'Macca seemed to have recovered from the worst of his off-field issues,' Kevin Gage recalled, 'while there was also a great experienced defender in Derek Mountfield with him, and we hadn't heard much about Kent Nielsen, a six-foot-four Dane, but he was such a good, strong defender and a great tackler. Those three didn't give the forwards much change and our wing-backs had the licence to get forward.

'As soon as we started playing that three-at-the-back system, everything fell into place and we all seemed to find our best form. With every win we started to gain in confidence, especially after that Everton result.

'We went to Chelsea on New Year's Day and won 3-0 on the back of home wins against Manchester

United and Arsenal. So, by that time a lot of the players started to think we could win the league.'

Mountfield agreed the three-man defence was a masterstroke by Graham Taylor but what struck him most was how natural the tactic felt given that McGrath had been missing for a month, and they had barely played that way before.

'Everything about the team just gelled and clicked, from us going to three at the back; big "Sticks" Ormondroyd shocking oppositions as you never saw six-foot-six left-wingers; Gordon Cowans' quality in midfield; David Platt coming of age and scoring goals for fun,' said Mountfield.

'Winning games becomes a habit and we got into a flow and the crowd and media started believing in us. Everything became a positive. We lost a few games we shouldn't have lost, but mostly it was all positive.

'The three at the back tactic was great for us. It was as if Graham realised, "Shit, I have three central defenders who are all playing really well. How do I fit them all in?" I have never played with defenders before where we all fitted so naturally alongside each other. Kent was the supplest player for his size that I have ever seen in my life, and Paul McGrath is the best player I have ever played with in my whole career. He was outstanding every time at three o'clock on a Saturday.

'We were in training one day and Graham stopped things and said, "Right, we're going to change things and go three at the back." Then we would try five at the back, then back to four, until he settled on the three-man unit with myself, Macca and Kent.

'He tried Stuart Gray and Kevin Gage both as left wing-backs, Chrissy Price went to right wing-back, he even tried Paul in midfield once, so he experimented with all kinds of plans before we settled on the formation that eventually worked well for us.

'When we went into a match with the three, it felt like we had played it for 20 years. It all felt so comfortable. We were very fluid with it, too. I might start on the left with Kent on the right and Macca in the middle, then I could go into the middle and Macca would be on the left. We interchanged quite a lot and it felt very natural. It wasn't a set formation; it was very fluid.'

Platt's goal contributions and late runs from midfield were a hallmark of Villa's season, along with the three-man defence and Nigel Spink's reliable goalkeeping, Tony Daley's pace on the wing, and the industry of Gage and Cowans in the middle of the park. His subsequent global breakthrough at the World Cup months later at Italia '90 changed his life, but his improvement could be traced back to this season of rapid progress.

'That Everton match was probably the start of David Platt's rise,' Gage suggested. 'The whole country was talking about Platty after this game and how he took his goals so well. Platty had such a good eye for goal with his late runs. Anything he touched that year just turned to gold.

'He wasn't a great box-to-box midfield player because quite often he would just run all over the place, wherever he wanted to run. He had Gordon Cowans and myself to do the leg work. Because Sid Cowans was such a good passer of the ball, I let him dictate the play and I just added a bit of grit, desire and energy in the midfield around him and Platty. But you couldn't knock Platty's ability to finish. He was brilliant for us that season.'

Mountfield went a step further and partly attributed Platt's growing effectiveness to Cowans, his silky midfield colleague who had already trod this path with Villa in 1981 as a league and, subsequently, European Cup winner in 1982.

'Platt was great, Macca was Macca – he hardly put a foot out of place, but for me the key to our success that season was Gordon Cowans,' Mountfield said. 'He sat there, dictated the play and gave Platty the licence to get forward. He was a magnificent footballer and I loved having him as a team-mate.'

Despite the turnaround in form, with the five-match win streak that culminated with the Everton match, and then the seven straight wins in the new year, manager Taylor never allowed himself to look too far ahead, even if the players were starting to believe that great things lay ahead.

'If you keep winning and are getting results,' said Stuart Gray, 'everyone is buoyant and it's great to go into training on a Monday morning. Graham was all about the next game, though. That's all he allowed us to focus on. That's how we prepared.'

6

Bloody Wimbledon, Again!

'They used to kick you up in the air and,
in those days, they got away with it a lot
more than they would now.'

– Ian Ormondroyd

VILLA'S SURGE to the top of the First Division did not come about from a lucky sequence of results at the start of the season, when a kind fixture list can sometimes skew the big picture.

It came in late February, and they were serious title contenders with just over two months of the campaign to run. The performance at White Hart Lane that had elevated them to the summit was sufficient evidence that they were where they deserved to be.

What came next, though, probably explained why their final league position was second, and not first.

A 3-0 home defeat to Wimbledon, followed by a 2-0 loss at Coventry City, was a bitter pill for Graham Taylor and his players to swallow and it exposed an innocence, a naivety, and certainly a lack of experience in getting the job done under the extreme pressure of a league title bid.

Kenny Dalglish's Liverpool, Villa's rivals at the top of the table, had been there and done it before. At least half a dozen of their squad had won the 'double' in 1986. Only Gordon Cowans and Derek Mountfield in Villa's line-up had experience of a title win.

The Reds did not self-destruct in quite the same way as Villa. Yes, they also had a battle on their hands against Wimbledon in the run-in but managed a 2-1 victory. They went to Coventry and although they conceded the first goal early on, the Reds then came back to win 6-1. That ruthlessness, and almost certainly the extra quality and squad depth, was the difference.

'That period, Wimbledon at home and Coventry away, rocked the boat and cost us in the run-in, which allowed Liverpool to catch us and jump ahead of us,' Stuart Gray admitted. 'We had back-to-back defeats later on at Palace and home to Man City as well, but I thought the Wimbledon game started our slide and eventually cost us the title.

'Every one of their players were well-drilled on how to master set plays. They all seemed to be three or four inches taller as well, which wasn't helpful as it was often an aerial game more against those guys than a game on the ground. It's a style of play that wins games if you play it well and they were masters of hitting 70-yard balls and winning the knock-downs.'

This defeat wasn't exactly a one-off bad day at the office against the Dons for Villa around this period. They lost ten of their 19 matches against them from the start of the 1986/87 season through to the beginning of 1994/95. That equates to 53 per cent of those fixtures being lost.

Wimbledon were a huge bogey team for Villa, so much so that Ron Atkinson was sacked after a 4-3 loss to them in 1994, even after his men had led 3-1. Wimbledon also knocked Villa out of the FA Cup on three occasions in that period, including a dramatic 6-5 penalty shoot-out triumph in the 1992/93 campaign.

Conversely, Villa played a strong Liverpool team on 16 occasions in the same period and lost just five times for a much lower 31 per cent loss ratio.

What was it about Wimbledon that made them such a difficult opponent? They were a team nobody wanted to play against. Their physicality, or crude aggression, their directness with long balls and long throws, their enthusiasm to drive the ball upfield and create mayhem in the opposition half, all made for a nightmare scenario. Why else would a great Liverpool team slip to a 1-0 loss in the 1988 FA Cup Final?

'They were old-school,' said Ian Ormondroyd. 'Rough, up and at you, they used to kick you up in the air and, in those days, they got away with it a lot more than they would now. They had a great team spirit and some good players as well. People talk about Vinnie Jones being rubbish, but he wasn't, he was decent. They had Dennis Wise, lots of decent players, they weren't a poor side. They played in a way that suited them.'

Kevin Gage had spent seven years at Wimbledon and was well aware of the famous Wimbledon spirit that helped christen them 'the Crazy Gang'.

'I can only speak of the time I was there, and we were very physical, especially after the signing of John Fashanu,' Gage acknowledged. 'He made a huge difference. We all knew our own games, we were good at set pieces, we had a lot of passion, enthusiasm and desire, and the manager Dave Bassett was a big part of that.

'On top of all that, we had some very good players. Dennis Wise, Nigel Winterburn, Glyn Hodges, and many more. It doesn't matter how aggressive and passionate you are, without good players, you're nothing, and to be fair to Bobby Gould he kept that going once Dave Bassett left.'

Gould orchestrated that Wembley triumph over Liverpool in '88 and also won four of his five matches against Villa as the Dons' boss. His side even beat Villa on all three occasions in the 1988/89 campaign.

Curiously, Gould said he always had a soft spot for Villa from his childhood, but it didn't prevent him from being ruthless as an opposition manager!

'I was a Coventry City supporter from childhood, but I would do my paper round in Coventry and always looked out for Villa's scores, because my dad took me there occasionally, and to St Andrew's, Molineux, and Filbert Street because I was in love with football and just liked to go to games all over the Midlands. So, from those early days I always had an affinity with Aston Villa.'

Gould's Coventry team even took four points off Villa in the 1992/93 season when Villa were trying to win the title again. Those results included a 3-0 win on Boxing Day. How does he explain his, and especially Wimbledon's, success over Villa?

'A lot was down to Don Howe,' Gould acknowledged. 'I took Don with me because he was one of the best individual coaches you could ever come across in that period. Some of the boys couldn't believe that the great Don Howe was coaching them at little old Wimbledon. But it was funny because they coached Don as well about the merits of long-ball football.

'I get pissed off nowadays with all the passing that goes on, yet teams don't seem to have gone anywhere. We had a direct approach whereby we delivered the ball into the attacking third and then squeezed everyone up to support the front men.

'We wouldn't allow them to be dirty as Don was a very clean professional as a player and coach. But obviously things went on out there that we never encouraged, as players couldn't help themselves at times.

'Me and Don also wanted pace in our play, so we went out and bought players like Terry Gibson, Carlton Fairweather was already there, so it blended well with what we were doing.

'It was a strange dressing room in terms of the various characters, like John Fashanu, Dave Beasant and Lawrie Sanchez, but they all came together and got on with it. They bonded and did the job as a team.

'John Fashanu up front was the big man for us. If we were in trouble, we would just keep hitting balls up to Fash as he would make things happen. Fash knew it and the other ten players knew it. "Get it up there to the big man, he'll battle for it, and we can work off the knock-downs." That was the message.'

On his battles against Graham Taylor's Villa, Gould added, 'It was always a challenge against Villa and it's interesting because Graham was known as the pioneer of the long-ball game so to beat him at his own game was a feather in our caps. But we did work hard at what we did. On Thursday afternoons nobody was allowed to go home until we had mastered all our dead-ball drills, so at about five o'clock they would then go home. Free kicks, corners, you name it, we practised it. But it was fun.'

That hugely damaging 3-0 loss at home to Wimbledon was all the more exasperating because David Platt missed a fifth-minute penalty. Fashanu made no such mistake when he had a spot kick in the second half, for his first of two goals on the day. The powerful centre-forward scored eight goals against

Villa in that period, and Ron Atkinson made him one of his last signings for the club in 1995.

'We played Sheffield Wednesday away earlier that season and I missed a penalty in a 1-0 defeat, or so it's said,' Stuart Gray reflected. 'But in fact, I caught my spot kick beautifully and I'm adamant it would have gone in off the post had their keeper Kevin Pressman not gambled and dived early to pull off what looked like a worldy of a save. It should have been retaken but it wasn't so, officially, my penalty was saved.

'Graham being Graham had a dig at me after that match and although I had a go back, saying how the keeper moved too early, he wasn't having it and he ended up taking me off penalties and putting Platty on them instead. I'm good friends with Platty still and I wind him up that he must have had a clause in his contract to be the penalty taker!'

'You would normally have put your mortgage on Platty scoring that spot kick,' Gage added, 'but he tried to hit it down the middle and Hans Segers never dived and had an easy save. So, from what should have been 1-0 to us and go on for a win, became a 3-0 hammering. What a nightmare that was.'

The subsequent defeat at Highfield Road allowed Liverpool to retake top spot in the league table.

Although the double blow of two consecutive losses was a serious dent to Villa's title bid, their slide was not yet terminal.

'I remember the Coventry game well – it was televised,' Derek Mountfield commented. 'I got injured just after half-time, my knee went clonk, Jim Walker came on and was rattling my knee around and I was rolling in pain. The referee was rushing him to decide as to whether I was staying on or going off. Jim told me to stay on for the corner and I didn't know it at the time, but a piece of floating bone was stopping my knee from extending.

'I stayed on, and Kevin Drinkell scored from the corner. I then went off and a minute later they went 2-0 up [through David Smith]. I spent the next week trying to get treated and ended up being operated on the day we played Oldham Athletic in the FA Cup.'

The Oldham match was another bitter blow, but first came a bounce-back victory over Luton Town at Villa Park that returned Villa to the summit once again.

The 2-0 win was much needed at a time when the Villa players' confidence was showing signs of shrinking in the face of Liverpool's steely temperament in their own title bid.

Tony Daley scored the first goal just before the half-hour, when he rampaged with speed and menace towards the Holte End and slotted in what he considers one of his best-ever goals.

'The pressure was on us, we needed a big performance,' Daley recalled. 'I remember seeing a banner in the Luton end saying "We'll stop the Daley delivery". I was getting a lot of good press then and teams were looking to stop me.

'It's one of the best three goals of my career. Gareth Williams slid the ball out to me just before the halfway line, then one of their defenders pulled my shirt and tried to foul me. I managed to get away from him and as I neared the byline I cut inside another defender. Then I quickly thought, "Do I cross it for Ian Olney? Err, no." And I poked it in past the keeper at his near post. It's one of my favourite goals along with my volley against Everton and the breakaway goal at West Brom in the FA Cup.'

Unfortunately, Villa's revival was short-lived. They had an FA Cup quarter-final against Oldham from the Second Division and although Joe Royle's team were certainly no pushovers on their plastic pitch, this was a game Villa were expected to win and progress through to the last four.

Oldham were League Cup runners-up that same season and were promoted to the top flight the season after. With players like Ian Marshall, Andy Ritchie and Earl Barrett, they posed a tricky challenge and Villa subsequently crashed to a 3-0 loss, which Taylor had no excuses for and admitted his side were well beaten.

'That was awful, and I was absolutely shocking that day,' Daley admitted. 'It was a great opportunity for us to kick on and have a good cup run.'

Oldham had eliminated Everton in the previous round after two replays and had also dumped Arsenal and Southampton out of the League Cup earlier in the campaign. So, Villa were in good company.

'Graham Taylor was very complimentary afterwards,' Oldham manager Joe Royle remembered. 'Most times we beat a big club at home the manager was usually quick to point out that our plastic pitch was the biggest factor. But Graham didn't seek excuses.

'He said people talk about the plastic pitch being a huge advantage, but it was a pink elephant; he made the point the reason we did well was because of the number of balls we delivered into the opposition box. Graham was a good guy, and I went on to work with him as coach of the England under-21s.

'That Villa team was very strong, throughout the side. But we had good players. There was a secret to playing on the plastic and it was having players who could handle the ball. Players who knew how to control and pass. We could play on it.

'Our recruitment around that time was top-class, even if I say so myself. We brought Denis Irwin in on a free transfer from Leeds, Andy Ritchie, Frankie Bunn, Nick Henry and Mike Milligan in midfield. So many of those players went on to good clubs. Ian Marshall, who could play centre-half or centre-forward, ended up at Ipswich. All these players made a difference. Rick Holden went to Man City, Earl [Barrett] obviously went to Villa.'

The Oldham slip-up was the latest poor result for Villa in a season that was quickly descending into a nightmare climax. Derek Mountfield didn't play at Boundary Park in the FA Cup, but he detected a change in mood around the club once the cup run came to a painful halt.

'I felt that Oldham game took a bit of momentum out of the club and the team,' said Mountfield. 'There was a real feelgood factor around the team. We were thinking, "Yeah, we're going for the league, we're in the quarter-finals of the FA Cup against a Second

Division team ..." Then we seemed to stumble after that. One game can really knock your confidence and that's what happened to us at Oldham.'

It was announced, on the same day Villa exited the FA Cup, that Republic of Ireland centre-forward Tony Cascarino had agreed to sign and become the club's most expensive player.

The Oldham defeat, though, was a serious blow and Villa carried the hurt into their upcoming league matches.

7

Doug Spends a Million, as Title Bid Falters

'I think Cas would be the first to admit it didn't really work out for him at Aston Villa. Graham Taylor, in hindsight, probably would have wished he just stuck with Ian Olney. I don't think Cas was mobile enough to fit into our system.'

– Kevin Gage

ASTON VILLA'S record capture of target man Tony Cascarino for £1m created a buzz of excitement around the club. Supporters were buoyed by the rare demonstration of ambition from chairman Doug Ellis.

The transfer was expected to embolden Villa's title prospects after a jittery period. The move, though, did not work for either player or club. Villa dropped too many soft points in games that genuine championship contenders would expect to have won. They lost to Crystal Palace and Manchester City, and shared 3-3 draws with Norwich City and Everton to close out the season. Liverpool won eight of their final 11 league matches.

Villa had been slow to follow the trend of English football's willingness to pay as much as £1m for a player, after Nottingham Forest signed Trevor Francis for such an amount first in 1979 and that British transfer record was subsequently superseded by Wolverhampton Wanderers, who paid £1.45m for Andy Gray off Villa later in that same year. Local rivals West Bromwich Albion sold Bryan Robson to Manchester United for £1.5m in 1981, preceding a slew of subsequent seven-figure moves.

There was a rumour around Villa then that Ellis was initially refusing to hand over such a large fee to Graham Taylor for Cascarino, but when HMRC came calling at Villa's door for a hefty tax payment, the Cascarino purchase conveniently enabled Ellis to offset his tax burden. Cascarino had some romance historically with Villa, having visited the stadium for a League Cup match with Millwall-supporting friends even though he wasn't a fan of the Lions.

'That was my first visit to a really big ground outside of London,' Cascarino said, 'so the Villa always stuck with me from that day [when Villa won 2-0 in 1976/77, with goals from Chris Nicholl and Brian Little].

'My next memory of Villa Park was the 2-2 draw on the first day of the [1988/89] season and I managed to score both goals for Millwall. We went 2-0 up after I scored two in three minutes.

'I'd played against Everton and Spurs for Gillingham in the cup, including a replay at Goodison, but that second visit to Villa Park seemed like a reminder to me of what a big club was all about.

'I thought it was a great club to join. I asked Graham Taylor at Doug's house when I was signing for Villa whether he was going to take the England job because it was well known that Bobby Robson was leaving after Italia '90 and there were rumours that Graham might be replacing him. He said, "No." I wanted to know that because I needed to know the manager who was signing me would still be there to do pre-season. I needed hard pre-season training to get the best out of me and I knew I would get that with Graham.'

Cascarino's debut was at the Baseball Ground against Derby County, as young striker Ian Olney was discarded to make way for the Republic of Ireland international. Villa won 1-0 courtesy of a second-half Ian Ormondroyd goal, but Cascarino felt he should have scored.

'I needed an early goal to get going and I almost did score with a great header,' he recalled. 'I really pinged it and it was heading into the bottom corner and somehow Peter Shilton, who was 40 years old by then, managed to keep it out. It was one of those "if only" moments. Strikers want to get going with goals early and I wasn't able to do that.

'It was obviously a big transfer fee for me, but I can't say I felt the weight of the price tag. It was more that I detected the excitement of the Villa fans after the club had spent all that money and I was just desperate to do well. I knew I was brought in to help us win the title and I realised if we didn't win it, people would naturally start doubting if that money was well spent.'

Villa were still top of the First Division after the next two games, which were both disappointing results. First came QPR at Loftus Road, where a late Kent Nielsen equaliser was needed to salvage a point, and then a Villa old boy committed them to a dreadful 1-0 loss at Crystal Palace.

Garry Thompson, a Villa supporter from childhood, had assisted Graham Taylor's promotion campaign but was sold against his will to Watford, before eventually turning up at Palace. It was his goal that helped dent Villa's title hopes, but he was merely doing his job, of course. Palace boss Steve Coppell was just what Thompson needed. He was a straight talker, and he became Thompson's favourite manager in his career, as he was able to rekindle the striker's love for football after losing his appetite for the game following his move away from Villa.

'Graham wanted me out the door, he was messing me about and he finally got rid of me,' recalled Thompson. 'I joined Watford and made my debut on Boxing Day [in 1988]. A year later, though, I ended up at Palace, which was an interesting tale.

'I had this phone call from a guy with a gravelly voice saying, "Hi Garry, it's Steve Coppell and I want to sign you for Palace." I was adamant it was Tony Coton taking the piss, so I said, "Fuck off TC, it's not funny," and I put the phone down. The phone went again, and the voice said it was Steve Coppell again. I said, "TC, it wasn't funny the first time – now just fuck off." Then the phone went again for a third time but on this occasion, it was the Palace club secretary saying Steve Coppell is trying to get hold of me and will I answer the phone?

'Next time Steve Coppell rang I couldn't do enough for him, and he explained that Ian Wright had broken his leg, and they wanted to sign me for the last nine league games to help them stay up. I was like, "Yes Mr Coppell, where do I sign?"

'Once I agreed to sign for Palace, I asked Steve who we were playing at the weekend. When he said "Aston Villa" I thought, "Lovely, Graham Taylor again!"

'I said hello to a few of the Villa lads before the game. But once we kicked off there were no friendships out there. Palace did what Palace did and smashed the ball upfield from the kick-off to put the keeper under pressure. Then we managed to take the lead and stay ahead.'

A long throw from another former Villa player, Andy Gray, created panic. Paul McGrath lost two headers to Mark Bright after a flick-on and Thompson managed to poke the ball over the line from five yards despite a challenge from Chris Price. It was a poor goal to concede, though Villa remained two points clear of Liverpool after the match but had played two games more.

'It was a tough game and both teams had chances to score,' Thompson said. 'I saw Graham Taylor after the game. Everyone knew there was bad feeling between us because he sold me from Villa when I wasn't that keen to go. He came over and shook my hand in front of the media to show he had no hard feelings. He leaned in to me and said, "Do you realise what you've done?" I said, "I'm gutted for Villa but delighted that it's fucked you!"

'I really was gutted for Villa, though, as they were good enough to have won the league that year, but they had a few too many bad results that cost them.'

Yet another defeat a week later, 2-1 at home to Manchester City, effectively drove the final nail into Villa's title bid. Liverpool were not making the same errors and instead continued to pick up wins.

Consecutive 1-0 victories at Arsenal and then at home to Chelsea were too little too late, even though Chris Price enjoyed his rare goal in front of the live television cameras at Highbury. As the runners-up position became more likely, the post-mortem focused on how Cascarino's late-season arrival had upset a settled team rather than boosted it. Ian Olney had been a significant reason for the momentum that took Villa to the top of the table, and it was a gamble by Taylor to banish him for Cascarino.

'I think Cas would be the first to admit it didn't really work out for him at Aston Villa,' Kevin Gage reflected. 'Graham Taylor, in hindsight, probably would have wished he just stuck with Ian Olney. I don't think Cas was mobile enough to fit into our system.

'Liverpool signed a striker called Ronny Rosenthal on loan and he scored seven goals in eight games and that really gave them a bit of a push towards the end of the season, when they didn't put a foot wrong. All their top players just clicked and got the job done.'

Several team-mates shared Gage's opinion, though it's a little harsh on Cascarino, who went on to have a highly successful career with Marseille and Nancy in France, from 1994 to 2000. He notched 61 league goals in 84 games for Marseille. Sadly, though, his goalscoring form at Villa was simply barren.

'I didn't score at Villa until my ninth game there and although I had played well in some matches, the goals didn't come initially. The lads started to call me "Ted" and I didn't understand why. In the end I had to take Paul McGrath aside and ask him, "Paul, why are they calling me Ted? I don't understand it." He then explained that there was a joke going round that Graham Taylor bought the wrong striker from Millwall and should have signed Teddy Sheringham!

'I knew I had to get goals for Villa to have a chance of winning the title. I played ten games in the run-in, and I only scored two goals. I thought to myself afterwards, "If I had contributed more, and maybe scored four or five, we could have won it."

'If I had scored those five goals to help us win the title it would have been a massive coup for everyone: myself, the club, the fans. The manager would have been justified in spending all that money. It didn't feel like that at the end of the season.'

Ian Ormondroyd accepted that Villa's performances dropped off when Olney made way for Cascarino, but he didn't wish to blame the sudden decline all on the new guy.

'Cas was a nice guy and I got on well with him,' he said. 'But for whatever reason our form did drop away a bit when he came. I don't think it was his fault or we should attach any blame to him, because he was a good player.'

'Ian's ball retention was better than most,' Stuart Gray added. 'He wasn't flash, but he popped up with goals. Once we signed Cascarino for big money he had to play so Ian sat out, which in hindsight might not have been the right thing for us. It was tough on both Ian and Cas to fill the boots left by Alan McInally. People will naturally make the point though that we were top of the league without McInally.

'The number nine shirt at Aston Villa is traditionally a big shirt to fill when you consider the names that have played that role down the years like Andy Gray, Peter Withe and so on, so Cas really needed to hit the ground running and sadly he wasn't able to do that.'

Alan McInally commented, 'Ian Olney is a great example of someone who might never have seen the light of day at Aston Villa had I not left for Bayern Munich. If I had stayed at Villa, Ian would almost certainly have spent the whole of the next season on the bench. He was learning under myself and Garry Thompson for two years. He was still very slight, but he developed into a good footballer.'

'Ian Olney didn't get the credit he deserved that season,' said Derek Mountfield. 'I thought he did a fantastic job to replace Alan McInally and the fact we never missed Macca was largely down to how well Olney did when he came in. He really did a good job leading the line for us.

'The signing of Cas did backfire on us a little because he was a different sort of player. It forced us to play in a different way. We had a shape, a style and a formation that worked for us with Olney. When Cas came in, we had to modify things. I don't know but maybe that was a turning point as to why we lost the league. It was Graham's decision and we had to respect it.'

So, it was decided: Liverpool were champions on 79 points, Villa had to make do with second on 70, while Tottenham finished a further seven points further back with 63.

It was still an incredibly successful campaign having almost been relegated a season prior, but when a club reaches the summit so near to the end of the season and yet fails to claim the big prize, it will always disappoint supporters, players, everyone.

Garry Thompson was not surprised to see the turnaround in Villa's fortunes from afar, despite being a key part of their promotion team only two years earlier.

'McGrath made all the difference,' Thompson said. 'I had played against McGrath since we were kids, when he became a defender from a midfielder. Every time I played against him, he either gave me a dead leg or kneed me in the balls. But he wasn't a dirty player; he was a fucking good player.

'When I knew that Villa had signed him, I thought, "Wow, that could make all the difference," because with Taylor's organisational skills, with the likes of Mountfield in the back four with Macca, Gordon Cowans and Platty in midfield, they always had goals in them, so I wasn't surprised they turned things around. I would have been surprised if they won it, but I did expect them to challenge.'

Stuart Gray felt they were light on experience in the big moments compared to chief title rivals Liverpool, 'We started the season just wanting to improve on the season before to be honest, but once you get on a roll you want to keep going and achieve as much as you can.

'Liverpool at that time knew how to get over the line. Maybe their added quality in depth and the budget they had that allowed them to do that gave them an advantage over us, but still they knew how to get the job done. We didn't have that experience to call upon.'

Derek Mountfield echoed Gray's sentiments and had seen it all before, from both sides of the fence as a league champion and a league also-ran.

'We lost the league by nine points in the end, but it never felt like Villa were nine points worse than them,' Mountfield admitted. 'Liverpool were not that much better than us that season. People might say now that Liverpool romped to the title, but they didn't.

'Liverpool were just very good at seeing seasons out. They did it when I was at Everton. They won 11 of their last 12 games [drawing at Sheffield Wednesday in the other] in '86 and still only beat us by two points. They were masters at closing seasons out strongly when they had to, they had done it for years.

'The expectation of having to get points in every game was new to most of those Villa players and it was probably new to Graham as well. If you had asked us at the time if we felt that pressure, to have to keep winning to pip Liverpool, we would probably have said, "No, we're loving it." But in all honesty, I'm sure that pressure was there in the back of everyone's minds without us realising it was there.'

1989/90 season:

League position: 2nd (of 20)

League Cup: third round (lost 1-0 at West Ham United)

FA Cup: quarter-final (lost 3-0 at Oldham Athletic)

Full Members' Cup: Northern final (lost 4-2 on aggregate to Middlesbrough)

Top scorers: David Platt 24; Ian Olney 11; Tony Daley, Derek Mountfield 8

8

The Fallout of Italia '90

'I wanted to go to Italy to pit my ability against the best players in the world week-in and week-out.'

– David Platt

ITALIA '90 was ultimately a near miss for England as they fell agonisingly short of a World Cup Final place after exiting in the semi-finals on penalties to eventual champions West Germany.

For Aston Villa, it had a more far-reaching legacy. They lost their manager, as Bobby Robson bowed out after his second World Cup finals, and they eventually lost their star goalscorer after he enjoyed a career-changing tournament.

David Platt's spectacular goal against Belgium to secure a quarter-final with Cameroon changed attitudes in a positive way towards England, but more, it also changed Platt's life. His fairy-tale moment could not have been more dramatic. He initially replaced Steve McMahon as a 71st-minute substitute. The game, at 0-0, went to extra time and was heading for penalties until Platt scored what must surely be the greatest goal of his career in the 119th minute to shatter Belgian hearts and send England into the last eight.

It was not only the circumstances of the goal that were dramatic – it was a stunner. Paul Gascoigne floated a free kick into Belgium's goal area where Platt allowed the ball to pass over his head before swivelling and volleying into the net at the far post. It was a moment wannabe footballers dream about.

His special tournament did not end there. He also scored England's opener against Cameroon in the quarter-final and then showed nerves of steel to score in the penalty shoot-out in the semi-final, and scored with a bullet header from 12 yards against Italy in the third-place play-off. His life would never be the same again.

Platt had to meet the world's media the following morning as they all scrambled to find out more about this 24-year-old Lancastrian. Thereafter, his name would be known the world over. In particular, the Italians were especially attracted to him. It seemed inevitable then that it was only a matter of time before he left Aston Villa for a move to the continent.

On returning home, not only was it confirmed that Graham Taylor would replace Robson, but there was also strong media speculation that Genoa were trying to sign Platt.

Doug Ellis spoke with Platt and confirmed that Genoa had attempted to sign him for a reported £4m fee, but he had informed the Italian club that his player was not for sale.

Platt, with three years remaining on his Villa contract, knew he could not force the move himself. He did not wish to alienate himself from the Villa supporters and his team-mates by 'acting up' but privately the seed was now sown for a move to Serie A. Especially after Gordon Cowans had also alerted Platt that Fiorentina were interested in him. No moves were subsequently forthcoming then, but Platt knew a career in Italy was not far away. Platt and his agent even hired an Italian interpreter, who was based in Wolverhampton, to handle all correspondence with Italian clubs that were interested.

'I now had an ambition to play in Italy,' Platt said of the time following the World Cup. 'It had originally been merely a dream during the time when one of my childhood heroes, Michel Platini, was playing for Juventus.

'Then, when Alan McInally moved to Bayern Munich, I realised that if I kept improving, I too could move abroad. The seven-week period I had just spent in Italy had whetted my appetite for more. I was in love with the food, clothes, way of life and, of course, the football … I wanted to go to Italy to pit my ability against the best players in the world week-in and week-out.'

While Platt committed to Villa for at least one more season, Taylor's departure was confirmed. His three seasons had been very successful: a promotion campaign back to the First Division; consolidation; and then an incredible season of over-achievement or at least exceeding the expectations of the most optimistic of Villa fans.

'Bobby Robson decided he would be standing down after the 1990 World Cup in Italy, and I had already been mentioned as a possible successor,' Taylor wrote in his 2017 autobiography. 'I'd been involved with the FA since running the under-18 team and, shortly after I joined Villa, Bobby asked me to take an England B team to play in Malta, so I would be lying if I said the idea of managing England did not appeal to me.'

Taylor was immensely proud to manage his country, but he was honest enough to acknowledge that his three-year tenure was a failure. England qualified for the 1992 European Championship in Sweden but were eliminated at the group stage. That was the time when Taylor attracted particularly cruel tabloid headlines, notably seeing his head fused with a turnip and that nickname stuck.

Villa fans were naturally upset that Taylor walked away from his job as the manager of their club but understood his opportunity was too good to pass up. However, he might have wished he stayed if he knew what was coming.

The Villa players appreciated him, especially for his man-management skills that were often unnoticed by those on the outside. He was a manager who players generally liked and wanted to play for, as had been the case at Lincoln City and Watford beforehand.

'I was really struggling when I hurt my knee in that second season [1988/89] under Graham,' Kevin Gage said. 'I was having one of my best seasons in the centre of midfield and then suddenly I was out injured, and I struggled to cope with how my football was taken away from me.

'Graham must have learned that I wasn't in a great place mentally and unbeknown to me while I was having treatment from the club, he went round to my house to see my wife and enquired with her how I was coping and told her if there was anything he could do she only had to ask.

'He said to her, "Don't tell Kevin I've been round, but it's important he doesn't worry about anything as it will all be fine. We'll take care of him and you as a family."

'In the end he called me into his office a couple of days later and said, "I didn't know whether to tell you this, but I have been round to see your wife," and after my initial alarm – "Oh really, why did you do that?" – he explained his rationale. I thought it was great that I had such an understanding manager who was checking on my welfare. I understood his reasons entirely and appreciated it.'

Taylor's caring nature was a far cry from how Ron Saunders might have acted in the same scenario. Those who played under Saunders often recall stories of how he never wanted to know injured players and would pretty much banish them to faraway places where they wouldn't be 'a distraction' to his fit players. That wasn't Taylor's way; he was something of a revolutionary in the 1980s in terms of his caring nature towards footballers.

'I have huge respect for Dave Bassett for what he did for me and the team at Wimbledon, but I think Taylor was a better man-manager,' Gage added. 'He had a bit more empathy. With Bassett it was my way or the highway. Taylor was prepared to listen and take a few more opinions on board.'

'He had a reputation for being a boring person and a long-ball merchant, but his knowledge of the game and man-management skills were fantastic,' Derek Mountfield commented. 'He knew how to treat people.

'My son had some health problems just after I joined Villa, and I got a phone call at the training ground to say I needed to go and see him at the Good Hope Hospital. He'd had something like 15 fits in 20 hours.

'Next morning I went back into training and Graham said, "What are you doing here?" I told him I was there for training. He said, "No you're not, your family is more important. Get back to that hospital. Your family needs you more than we do." That will stick in my mind for ever. A lot of football managers treat you as a commodity, but Graham treated you as a person.'

Taylor's captain at Villa, Stuart Gray, was equally impressed with Taylor for his psychology skills as well as his tactics.

'I have been lucky enough to work under three great managers in Brian Clough, Graham Taylor and Glenn Hoddle,' Gray said.

'What floats my boat, though, might not necessarily float another player's boat. That's where clever man-management comes in and the best know how to get the best out of all their players, in different ways.

'It's all about getting the right balance between knowing who needs a kick up the arse, who needs a cuddle, who needs dropping, who needs telling the truth. You want all 11 players going on the pitch in the best possible frame of mind and a lot of clever man-management must go into reaching that scenario, which is where Graham was top-class.

'I wouldn't say we were a flamboyant team under him, but we were well-drilled, we all knew our jobs, we had round pegs in round holes, and Graham managed to get the best out of everybody.'

Ian Ormondroyd noticed Taylor's instinct as a tactician more than anything, and therefore felt sympathy for him when his name was eventually dragged through the proverbial coals as a target of the angry English football media.

'Graham got stick from his time with England, but I always spoke up for him, he was superb,' said Ormondroyd. 'He was organised, you always knew what he wanted from you, and he was so good tactically. The times we were losing a game, and he would just change things, maybe by making a substitution, and we'd end up winning, it's incredible. He was very instinctive and proactive at changing a game.'

Club secretary Steve Stride said it was common knowledge at Villa that if Taylor was offered the England job, he 'would jump at it' because it was one of his ambitions. However, no succession plan was ever put in place to deal with his eventual resignation.

'It all happened pretty quickly, we hadn't got a replacement lined up,' Stride recalled. 'If we had known a few months in advance, we would have put all our energies into finding a replacement. There was nobody in the frame initially to replace Graham.

'It was a shame he left us as things were brilliant. Promotion in his first year, runners-up to Liverpool two years later, who would have thought? Graham did a tremendous job. Not only on the pitch but he sorted things out off the pitch as well, such as the training ground, player contracts, and more. Then he was off.'

Doug Ellis sounded out a few managers before hiring Taylor's eventual successor. Tony Cascarino revealed how his Republic of Ireland manager Jack Charlton was approached by Ellis around the time of the 1990 World Cup.

'Jack told me when I was away with the Ireland squad that he could have been my manager at Villa, as he'd had a phone call from Doug about the job before Jozef Vengloš got it,' Cascarino explained. 'Jack turned it down, though, because he felt there was still a lot of legs left in the Ireland team.

'Jack had a successful campaign at Italia '90 and he was enjoying his role with Ireland, which suited his lifestyle as a part-time manager.

'I think, though, Jack would have been perfect for the Villa with the way the team was set up then. He and Graham were quite similar with the way they played, getting the ball wide and playing football further up the field.

'Both Jack and Graham hated giving soft goals away in terrible areas, like we see more of nowadays with the playing out from the back. They both liked the idea of a big striker leading the line, like I did for both of them, and with the midfield pushing on towards the strikers. They were also excellent man-managers. If you were on their side, they were great with you.'

9

The Dr Jo Experiment

'I thought Vengloš was quite incredible. I was just out of my teen years and wasn't drinking and I understood where he was coming from, but for everyone else it was a big uproar as English football was not used to his methods to instil more professionalism.'

– Dwight Yorke

GRAHAM TAYLOR was gone and there was no replacement on the horizon.

Jack Charlton had rebuffed Villa's approach and Oldham Athletic did not allow the club permission to speak to their manager Joe Royle. Media speculation also linked Villa with an audacious approach for World Cup-winning coach Franz Beckenbauer, though that seemed more like Doug Ellis's self-propelled PR machine at work than anything of substance.

'I knew Doug Ellis very well because my villa in Majorca was close to his,' explained Joe Royle. 'We went out on his boat a few times. For all the criticism he used to get, I liked him and thought he was a good guy. But I didn't find out that Villa wanted me until it all went away.

'My chairman at Oldham, Ian Stott, later told me that Villa had asked to speak to me, and he flatly refused them permission. The Villa job would certainly have interested me as I had already turned down Manchester City. He didn't tell me about Villa's interest until I was going to Everton about four years later in 1994. If I had known, who knows what might have happened?

'There are some clubs in the top flight who I didn't much care for, but I always thought Aston Villa was a big, big club and they were always very friendly and treated oppositions in a nice way.'

From nowhere, Ellis had a call from his friend Stuart Webb, who was secretary, chief executive and chairman in his time at Derby County. Webb had connections in Czechoslovakia and advised Ellis that Jozef Vengloš was available. The Czech national team had just been quarter-finalists at Italia '90 so he had a reasonable CV. Vengloš had also helped Czechoslovakia win the bronze medal at the 1980 European Championship.

An English top-flight club had never employed a foreign manager before and if there was one thing about Ellis that people close to him knew, it was that he loved being first at doing something notable. He loved telling anyone who would listen that he invented the bicycle kick, though there is less authenticity in that story than him becoming the first English club chairman to take on a manager from overseas.

'I was away on holiday during the interview process,' club secretary Steve Stride recalled, 'but soon received a phone call from Doug saying, "I have appointed the ex-Czech manager, Jozef Vengloš." I thought, "Oh, OK." But in truth the name didn't mean much to me.

'We then had his press conference to unveil him to the media and Doug opened the proceedings by announcing, "Gentlemen, I'm sure you all know who this is, our new manager Jozef Vengloš." There were a lot of blank faces, head scratching, and murmurings of, "Who's this guy?" No one knew who he was – maybe one or two did, but most didn't.

'There would certainly have been an element of ego here as Doug loved to go round saying he was the one who brought the first foreign manager into English football.'

Vengloš was unveiled to the media in July 1990. He signed a two-year contract with a 'break' clause meaning any of the two parties could get out if they wanted. Vengloš opted not to bring in any of his own staff and in hindsight this was seen as a huge mistake as he often cut an isolated figure.

The Vengloš experiment was ultimately a massive, almost costly, failure, and he departed on 29 May 1991, after offering his resignation a month earlier. Having been runners-up to Liverpool in the 1989/90 season, Villa only just avoided relegation under Vengloš.

With the same team that almost won the First Division, Villa finished fourth from bottom in a season in which two went down as the Football League was streamlined before the Premier League was introduced two years later. Villa's 41 points would have relegated them a season earlier when Sheffield Wednesday dropped with 43 points.

Very little went right for the Czech: Villa conceded five goals in three separate hammerings in the last six weeks of the season, to Arsenal, Manchester City and

Leeds United. Scant consolation came in David Platt's continued form, as he scored 24 goals in the campaign, and a spectacular 2-0 home win in the UEFA Cup against Italian powerhouses Inter Milan. Villa still exited the competition after a 3-0 away leg defeat.

Vengloš signed three players: Ivo Staš from Baník Ostrava – he never played a single game after sustaining a career-ending injury; Neil Cox joined for £425,000 from Scunthorpe United; and Gary Penrice was signed for £500,000 from Bristol Rovers. He also tried to buy Vinny Samways from Tottenham Hotspur but was unable to do so.

Villa's European Cup match-winner Peter Withe joined Vengloš in January 1991 as his assistant, though the move also flopped. Withe believed his role was different to what it had been officially described as. He felt more like the manager and deemed Vengloš more interested in coaching than performing the usual responsibilities associated with being a manager, like media interviews and team meetings.

Kevin Gage said the players found out about Vengloš's appointment during a pre-season tour.

'John Ward came over to us in training and said, "Right lads, your new manager is ..." and he got this piece of paper out of his pocket and said, "Jozef

Vengloš." We all looked at each other and went, "Who the fuck is Jozef Vengloš?" No one had any idea of who he was until it was pointed out that he had managed so and so.

'In fairness to the players, there was a bit of trepidation about what to expect from Vengloš, but nobody said, "I'm not having him." We were all prepared to give him a chance. But, pretty soon, it became obvious that his limited grasp of English was not going to be good enough to cope with a squad of predominantly English players.

'He just couldn't get over to the lads what he was trying to do. I can only speak for myself, and I didn't buy into it at all. I couldn't understand what he wanted. It was a mishmash of methods and communication. His training was a bit weird, and we just didn't click as a team under his management.'

The shared consensus among the players was that Vengloš was a nice guy who clearly knew the game but his communication skills, predominantly his poor command of the English language, meant that he was never going to be a success.

'It was a very strange appointment,' said Derek Mountfield. 'None of us knew who he was. Tactically he was very good, but he was extremely poor at getting his message over to us. He couldn't talk the language and we struggled to understand what he was trying to say. The language barrier between our English and his broken English was huge. Even his coaching staff didn't understand what he was trying to get over to us.

'He didn't change the team much either and players knew they could have a bad game and not really worry about losing their place in the side.'

Steve Stride thought Venglоš was too nice to be a manager at Villa, lacking the confidence in his own abilities and certainly the conviction to execute his coaching skills and ideas.

'Jo was such a nice bloke,' Stride commented, 'that I can understand why Doug liked having him as manager because he was too nice. It allowed Doug to have an element of control over football matters.

'Every Friday morning, Jo would come into the office and tell Doug his team. One day Doug wasn't there, and he told me the team and asked if I was happy with it. I thought to myself, "Jo, you're the manager, it doesn't matter what I think. That's what we pay you to do." He was way too nice and was so keen to please and do a good job that it went against the authority he was supposed to have at the club.'

One area where Vengloš encountered particular opposition from the players was around diet and nutrition. He did not want his players to drink alcohol at all and requested that they eat responsibly as he felt professional footballers should dedicate as much focus on this as their football. Peter Withe tried to advise Vengloš that he was too stringent in his efforts to eradicate alcohol from the players' diet, but the manager was adamant.

Stride added, 'Jo didn't understand the mentality of British players and apart from Dwight Yorke and Kent Nielsen they were all British. These are guys who might sometimes stop at the roadside café on the way to Bodymoor Heath and have a bacon and egg sandwich before training. And there was Jo trying to instil into the players the need for good diet and nutrition. Jo could never understand why, after a game, the players would go into the lounge and have a couple of pints and be laughing and joking whatever the result. If we had lost a game, Jo would be miserable for days. This was a move that was never going to work.'

Dwight Yorke, who was still adapting to life in England as a young pro after transitioning from the backwaters of Trinidad and Tobago, was in the minority among the squad as someone that was happy to embrace the manager's philosophies.

'The changes were immense, and life soon became very different around the club,' Yorke said. 'Graham Taylor was the father figure responsible for picking me up before dropping me off [Yorke smiles as he speaks], though I understood his reasons for him taking the England job as it seemed an opportunity he felt he couldn't refuse. But for a time, it felt like he had left me behind and there was no one to guide me and I had to adjust to that very quickly.

'I thought, though, that Vengloš was quite incredible. I was just out of my teen years and wasn't drinking and I understood where he was coming from, but for everyone else it was a big uproar as English football was not used to his methods to instil more professionalism.'

Tony Daley was another who appreciated Vengloš and his attempts to change the culture on and off the field at Villa Park.

The fact Daley became a strength and conditioning coach in his life beyond playing football shows that he was attuned to how players could make more of their abilities. Vengloš may have had some influence there.

'I can only say positive things about him,' Daley said. 'I learned a lot from him about how to look after yourself, how to conduct yourself, how to be a better professional externally away from football, such as things like eating and drinking right, taking care of your body in the right way, stretching before and after games.

'He was ahead of his time because there was still a "work hard, play hard" mentality in English football then. It changed a few years later. But at that time the players didn't really buy into his methods as he tried to ban alcohol and certain unhealthy foods. He wasn't appreciated by most of the players, but I was all over what he was saying.

'I made my England debut during the Venglоš era, so he did well for me even though his time was disappointing for the club.

'When English football, or specifically Arsenal, embraced what Arsène Wenger was doing it coincided with better results so that kind of radical approach was always going to be an easier buy-in with things going well on the field.'

Yorke and Daley were in a minority as far as players went who enjoyed the 'Venglоš way'. In fact, most players found the Czech's methods strange, especially his conditioning ideas in training.

'He was a nice person and I had a lot of time for him as a man,' Tony Cascarino commented. 'But I felt early on that the club was going to go backwards while he was at the helm. He was ahead of his time in terms of what he was preaching to us about diet and nutrition. But British football then was not ready for someone like him.

'I remember one of his early training sessions that was really weird. We had been doing some running and he asked us to put our fingers on our pulses on our neck. We were told you had to get to a certain number and of course everyone was lying. The lads were just shouting out, "Yeah, I've got 95," "I've got 110." It was supposed to be telling us about our heart, but the lads didn't have a clue what they were meant to be doing really. Most of us were being dishonest just to please him.'

The major highlight in an otherwise miserable season was the first leg against Inter Milan in the second round of the UEFA Cup at Villa Park on 24 October 1990.

The ban on English clubs' participation in Europe was lifted ahead of that season and Villa were one of the first to return to continental action. Vengloš famously said, 'Europe has been missing English teams. It has been like bread without butter.' FA chairman Bert Millichip quipped the ban had placed English football in a dark tunnel and the return was like sunshine coming back.

Villa had first beaten Slovakian side Baník Ostrava 5-2 on aggregate, which had brought Ivo Staš to their attention and eventually resulted in his transfer. He was seen as a Franz Beckenbauer-type player, who could operate in the centre of defence or in a deep-lying midfield role. His subsequent injury led to the trivia question, 'Which Aston Villa player scored for the club without playing a game?' The question referred to his 59th-minute own goal that gave Villa the winner in Ostrava.

Inter Milan would be a significant challenge. They possessed the German trio of World Cup winners Lothar Matthäus, Jürgen Klinsmann and Andreas Brehme, as well as seasoned Italy internationals such as 1982 World Cup winner Giuseppe Bergomi, goalkeeper Walter Zenga, Nicola Berti and Riccardo Ferri.

Villa took the lead in the 14th minute after Cascarino teed up the big number six Kent Nielsen to fire in a first-time shot from 20 yards with his trusted right foot that gave Zenga no chance.

The Villa team that lost 3-0 to Inter Milan in the San Siro, after taking a 2-0 lead from Villa Park.

Jozef Venglos speaks with striker Tony Cascarino, during a difficult season for him in which he only narrowly avoided relegation with Villa.

David Platt's dramatic extra-time goal against Belgium for England at the 1990 World Cup changed his life and ultimately sparked his subsequent move to Bari in Serie A.

Doug Ellis finally hired Ron Atkinson as manager in 1991, at the third time of trying, but their relationship was far from harmonious.

Kevin Richardson (left) and Steve Staunton, pictured here with Wolves' Steve Bull, were two of Ron Atkinson's first signings in a frantic summer of transfer activity in 1991.

Dwight Yorke was Villa's top scorer in Big Ron's first season as manager, but he largely played a supporting role to senior players like Cyrille Regis, Tony Daley, Dalian Atkinson and Dean Saunders, until Brian Little took over as boss.

Dean Saunders and Ray Houghton celebrate with Dalian Atkinson after his goal of the season at Wimbledon in the 1992/93 season.

Australian goalkeeper Mark Bosnich saves yet another penalty to help send Villa to Wembley in the 1994 League Cup Final.

Villa won their first major trophy in 11 years at Wembley in 1994 after defeating Manchester United 3-1 in the League Cup Final. No league title, but it was still silverware!

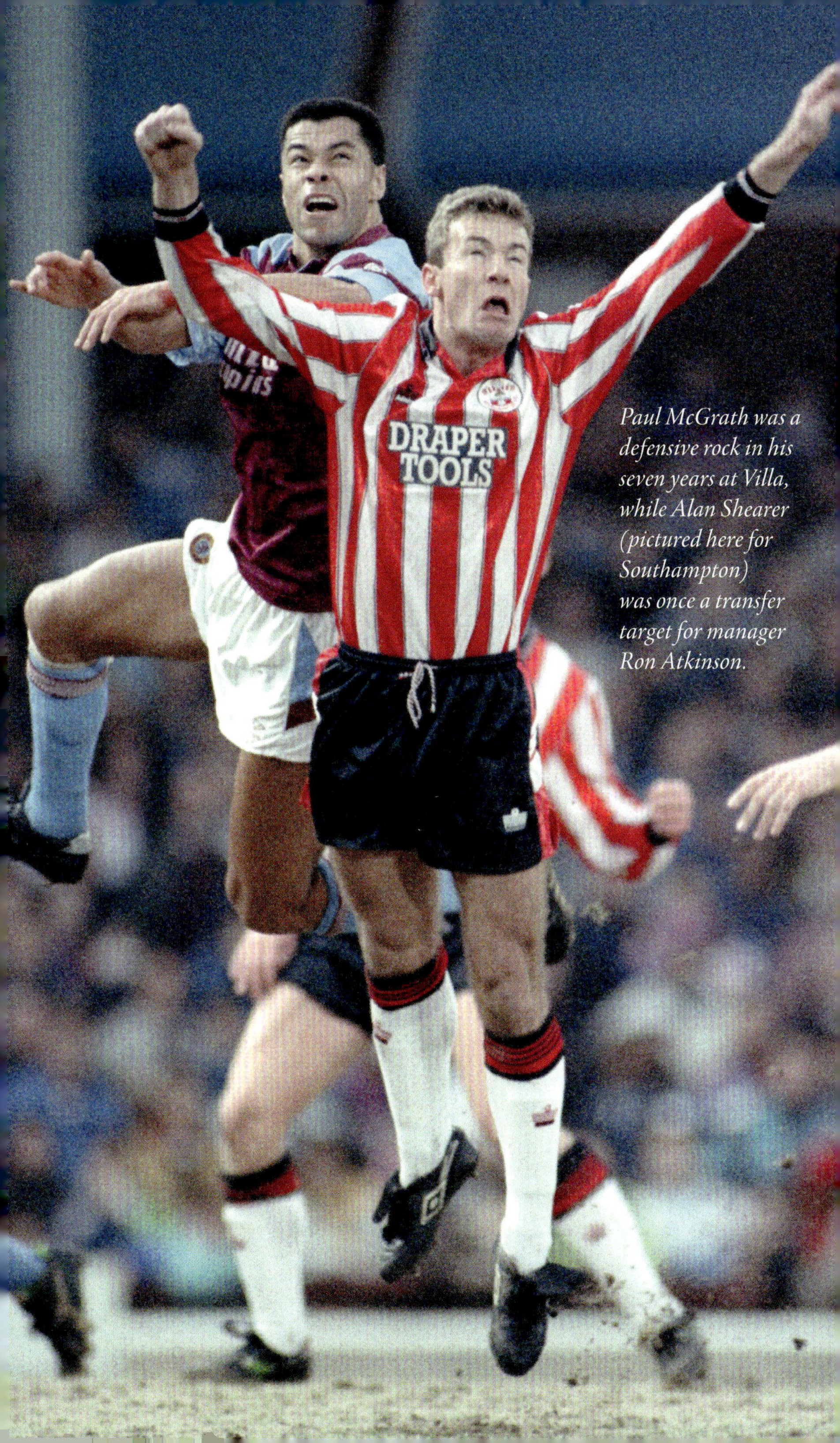

Paul McGrath was a defensive rock in his seven years at Villa, while Alan Shearer (pictured here for Southampton) was once a transfer target for manager Ron Atkinson.

Tony Daley, one of the greatest entertainers in Villa's history, won two league championship runner-up medals under Graham Taylor and then Ron Atkinson.

Villa's league title and European Cup winners in 1981/82 still reign supreme in terms of their winning legacy. For now.

They doubled their lead midway through the second half when a signature pass of quality from Gordon Cowans found David Platt's run towards the Inter goal. He controlled Cowans' chip perfectly with his right foot and then dinked it past Zenga at his near post. It was yet more Platt success in front of a widespread Italian audience that added further weight to the probability that a move to Serie A was inevitable.

'I received a great deal of glory for the way that I finished that move off, but for me the best part of it was Sid's pass,' Platt acknowledged. 'It is my firm belief that Sid helped me get into the England team and helped to keep me there. Of the 68 goals I scored for Aston Villa, he was responsible for making approximately 70 per cent of them. His range of passing with either foot was unbelievable; this, coupled with his vision, meant he invariably gave me three efforts on goal per game. During my time at Villa, I was once asked what my ambition was. I joked that it was to make a run that Gordon Cowans didn't see.'

Villa's optimism surrounding an unlikely triumph in the UEFA Cup tie was extinguished at the San Siro when Inter bounced back with a 3-0 win.

In front of a crowd of 75,580, Villa capitulated to the worst possible start by conceding a goal in the sixth minute. It was a sloppy goal, too, as a hopeful long ball from Inter's defence really should have been dealt with by Villa's three-man backline. Instead, Klinsmann managed to squeeze between Nielsen and Mountfield and somehow bundle the loose ball past goalkeeper Nigel Spink. The second and third goals came after half-time and Villa's hopes were dashed.

'We battered them at Villa Park and it was our best performance of the season,' Cascarino recalled. 'I remember thinking, "These guys are not very good." And then you learn about European football because we went to their place and they were completely different.

'I had a header that struck the crossbar that would have made it 1-1 and although it was a good header I remember thinking, "Wow, what a big miss that was." They ripped us apart and were a totally different team to how poorly they had played at Villa Park.

'It felt like a huge punch on the nose at their place after we had played so well at Villa Park, when Tony Daley was unplayable. Dales had his best performance that I ever saw him have that night, they couldn't cope with his pace. He was lightning quick.'

Stuart Gray added, 'To lead the team out at Villa Park and at the San Siro and to beat them 2-0 at home, these are memories that sit in the top five memories of my whole career. The noise at Villa Park was the loudest I have ever heard at a match I've been involved in.

'The 3-0 loss at the San Siro, though, will for ever be a scar on my memory as we were 2-1 up on aggregate at half-time in the second leg but couldn't see it out. So, one of my greatest highs was followed by a huge low.'

Derek Mountfield concluded, 'The home leg was a massive high in that season, before a massive low at the San Siro. The win at Villa Park was one of the best atmospheres I witnessed as a player in my whole career and will stay with me for ever, as I'm sure is the case for the other lads. It was just a shame we couldn't finish off the job at their place, but the refereeing wasn't great. I'll leave it at that.'

10

Vengloš Out, Big Ron In

'Vengloš got shut down quite quickly by the players as the drinking culture in England then was apparent. His attempted changes were too severe for the players and when there is so much wrangling between the team and the manager, there is only going to be one winner and the player power shut him down.'

– Dwight Yorke

JOZEF VENGLOŠ was not disliked as a man by the Aston Villa players – on the contrary; but as a coach they would not entertain his methods to revolutionise their culture. Whatever ideas he had about tactics they just did not understand.

The communication breakdown between players and manager was so extreme that the relationship was only ever destined to fail. His one season in English football will be remembered as a stinker of a campaign, but he was mostly misunderstood. Maybe his biggest mistake was not appointing better support staff who could not only persuade the players to buy into his methods but also help create the kind of happy, feel-good work environment that a coach like Steve Harrison did for Graham Taylor with his ideal combination of supreme coaching skills and a wicked sense of humour.

Vengloš often cut a worrisome, lonely figure and although his wife came over, club secretary Steve Stride said he cannot remember anyone ever taking him out socially, which was unusual in the world they existed in.

'I felt sorry for him on a number of occasions,' Stride said. 'We got off to a bad start and never recovered.

'Jo was unlucky. Whatever he touched turned to stone and Ivo Staš was a great example of that. He played against us for Baník Ostrava in the UEFA Cup, and he stood out as an outstanding player. He looked like another Beckenbauer and we quickly paid half a million to bring him to Villa. Then in his first week of training, he did his Achilles and never played football again! How unlucky is that?'

Vengloš gave Dwight Yorke his full debut, at Manchester United on 29 December 1990, a 1-1 draw that saw a Steve Bruce penalty and a Gary Pallister own goal to draw Villa level. Yorke never forgot that and has been thankful to Vengloš ever since. He felt sympathy for Vengloš having witnessed clear opposition to his coaching philosophy by his team-mates.

'I got baptised at the Theatre of Dreams against the likes of Paul Ince, Bryan Robson and Mark Hughes,' Yorke said. 'It was quite incredible and another step in my development. I felt like I was making huge strides forward, though Villa fans might not have seen that by then, as I had the likes of Tony Daley and Nigel Callaghan still ahead of me.

'Jozef Vengloš was great for me. But he got shut down quite quickly by the players as the drinking culture in England then was apparent. His attempted changes were too severe for the players and when there is so much wrangling between the team and the manager, there is only going to be one winner and the player power shut him down.

'It was a shame as Dr Vengloš was a good coach, but the boys didn't buy into it, which explained the drop-off in performance from the time he took over from Graham Taylor.'

It was not only the alcohol and fast-food bans that Vengloš attempted to implement which marginalised him with the squad. Most of the players were often baffled by his coaching ideas much of the time.

'He couldn't speak English well and he just muddled along with no interpreters,' Ian Ormondroyd recalled. 'He couldn't get his message across, and the players were quite down on him.

'His training methods were proper weird, as he'd tell us things like, "Run for a hundred yards and hold your breath!" Training sessions should be fun, but they weren't. We kept questioning why we were doing things. It was very different to what Graham had done as he was very clear in what he wanted from us. Vengloš just didn't work, though I know he had a decent track record in international football.'

Tony Cascarino was especially down on Vengloš because he had hoped to work longer with the manager who signed him only months earlier, Graham Taylor. The striker adamantly felt he was at his best following a gruelling pre-season to raise his fitness levels and he felt cheated out of that with Vengloš's arrival on hearing the way Taylor worked his players in pre-season.

'The players were pulling out all the stops to get results for Dr Jo and the fact it never happened for us, I think, just showed we were huge over-achievers the season before,' Cascarino said.

'There was the constant inevitability throughout the Vengloš season that Platty was going; no one knew if Vengloš would survive; everything seemed to be uncertain and up in the air. It felt like we were a sinking ship, and players were trying to sort themselves out with lifeboats.

'The players never bought into him. On a pre-season tour in Hong Kong, Jo gave us a big talk about what he expected of us and halfway through [physio] Jim Walker whispered in his ear, and then Jo said to Jim, "Do I really need to say that?" And Jim said, "Yes, you do." He then told us we can't go out drinking. But, of course, we did. We were all in Joe Bananas. It wasn't an Aston Villa problem though, as English football generally had a booze culture then, whether you were at Arsenal, Liverpool or Manchester United. That was how it was, and Jozef Vengloš struggled to accept it.'

'Nobody hated Jozef Vengloš,' Kevin Gage said. 'We respected him as the manager, he was happy and smiley around the place. But on the training pitch or in the dressing room, anything he tried to implement in terms of his tactics went horribly wrong.

'I was a professional and was motivated to try and do well. But the spark that was around the squad under Graham Taylor just wasn't there with the new management. A lot of Vengloš's team-talks were painful because he wasn't able to get his points across and you could sense his frustration. He would sometimes use flipcharts and magnetic markers on a board but it still wasn't easy to follow his tactics.

'There was one famous incident on a trip to Kuala Lumpur when he read out his team, going through all the different positions, and went on for five minutes about how Gareth Williams had a crucial role in this game. Me and Stuart Gray looked at one another and smiled as we realised what was happening and we couldn't help chuckling. Then Stuart put his hand up and said, "Boss, you haven't picked a goalkeeper, you've got 11 outfield players." Quick as you like, Vengloš said, "Oh yes, Gareth, you sit out." After minutes telling us how big a role Gareth had. It was hilarious. I can't believe an established international manager could spend all afternoon thinking about his team and then name his side – without a goalkeeper. It was embarrassing.

'And I don't think it helped Vengloš that his number two was the club legend Peter Withe, who was very strict and sergeant major-like with the players. He grated on quite a few of the boys and that might be hard for some Villa fans to digest given he's an absolute legend as a Villa player – but he didn't work as a coach. It wasn't a successful move at all.'

Withe's appointment was meant to appease the supporters in one way after the Vengloš move had started badly. He stayed on with the first team until Vengloš departed that summer.

Many believe Withe should have better advised Vengloš that the team was not as strong as he might have thought having taken them on after finishing as runners-up to Liverpool. The common belief is that Graham Taylor performed a miracle to have that squad finish so high.

It was a clear case of over-achieving, a team punching above its weight. As an outsider, though, it would have been difficult for Vengloš to have understood that.

Stuart Gray felt Vengloš was not helped by Withe, who Vengloš allowed to police the squad in what Gray felt was an often unnecessarily spiky manner.

'I had a lot of time for Vengloš,' Gray said. 'I was captain of the team, and he relied a lot on me to get his message across, which wasn't always easy.

'Graham Taylor was excellent in regards to man-management because he would dig out the best player in the team and give him a rollicking in front of everyone, whether that be Alan McInally, David Platt or whoever, but he would then put his arm around them in the next breath and so was able to soften the message in a way that didn't alienate the players.

'Peter, though, would dig players out and I would say he went over the top at times and was over-aggressive. Some of the best players then started to think, "Hang on, what's going on here?" It was a very different style of management, which is a very personal thing.'

Gray added, 'Having finished runners-up the season before, it was very disappointing to stay up by the skin of our teeth.

'Under Graham we were a squad that knew what was expected of us every day, but with Vengloš we just didn't understand what he wanted us to do. The team needed improving and freshening up also, but Doug probably thought after finishing second the team didn't need any money spending on it!'

Derek Mountfield observed how Villa were used to winning so often in the season before, but quickly became accustomed to doing too many things wrong under Vengloš.

'It became a difficult habit to break,' he said, 'which wasn't good for us as individuals or as a team. We should have pushed on from what we had done the season before, but we didn't and that was very disappointing.'

Gage recalled the final game in the Vengloš reign at Villa Park as a telling moment regarding how far the club had slipped in a year. They drew 2-2 at home to Chelsea having trailed 2-0 after just four minutes.

What alarmed Gage most was the way some fans carried Mountfield on their shoulders at the final whistle as if the club had won a cup or achieved promotion. He saw it as a sorry indication at how supporters' expectations had been lowered in the space of one season.

'Some of the players thought it was weird having just missed out on relegation,' said Gage.

Peter Withe tried to persuade Vengloš to stay on at Villa for another season but the feeling from Vengloš and indeed the chairman was that it was the right time for the coach to leave the club.

'I heard Jo say on several occasions to Doug, "Mr Chairman, if you are not happy with me, it is not a problem,"' Steve Stride revealed. 'I seem to recall he was on a two-year contract but when he left, he said, "I have not succeeded, I have failed, you don't need to pay me [anything]." But we gave him 25 grand and he was happy.'

Vengloš's eventual successor, Ron Atkinson, had known him since the early 1980s, from when he had been commentating at international matches. Atkinson counselled Vengloš on how he should navigate his exit out of Villa.

'He was a nice bloke, maybe too nice,' Atkinson said. 'I remember telling him after I saw him at Villa Park when Whitey [David White] scored four as Villa lost 5-1 at home to Man City, I said don't let that chairman persuade you to resign, you get yourself a pay-off!'

Atkinson had no clue at that stage he would end up succeeding Vengloš. He had just signed a new contract at Sheffield Wednesday after leading them to promotion back to the top flight in the same season as securing a shock League Cup Final win at Wembley over his former club Manchester United. He had no intention of leaving Hillsborough – he was happy there. But if there was one club that was likely to tempt him, it was always going to be Villa.

Atkinson, whose family relocated from Liverpool to Birmingham when he was a child, had spent three years in the youth system at Villa from 1956 to 1959, rubbing shoulders with the likes of Peter McParland, Johnny Dixon and Gerry Hitchens. However, he never played a single first-team game and instead spent his entire playing career at Oxford United.

Villa had attempted to make Atkinson their manager in 1984 before appointing Graham Turner, but at that time he was in the hot seat as Manchester United boss and, understandably, wasn't prepared to give up that opportunity. Doug Ellis also asked Atkinson to leave Wednesday for Villa once it was known that Graham Taylor was taking the England job in 1990. At that stage, though, Atkinson felt obligated to Wednesday as they had just been relegated to the Second Division and he wanted to do the decent thing and attempt to win promotion at the first time of asking, which he managed to achieve.

'That whole experience of getting Ron out of Sheffield Wednesday wasn't pleasant as he had won a cup with them, got them promoted and they really didn't want him to go,' Steve Stride remembered. 'There was not much they could do about it, though, and we just had to come to a settlement.

'But even Ron played hard to get for a while. The chairman and I went to Ron's house in Barnt Green, and by the time we left he still hadn't signed. Later that day we had a call from Ron's wife, Maggie, saying Ron will join Villa but we should increase his signing-on fee. I am not sure that Ron never had any knowledge of that call as we were meant to believe but, anyway, we did increase the offer, and he did eventually sign.'

Peter Withe had by then been appointed reserve team manager, so Atkinson brought in Andy Gray as his assistant to achieve a clean break from the Vengloš era. John Ward subsequently left the club.

Withe's first main assignment under Atkinson was to get Nigel Callaghan fit during pre-season after Withe had identified the state of the winger's fitness, which was supposedly unacceptable. Withe, though, did not serve the Atkinson regime for long and left in October 1991 to take the Wimbledon job.

Andy Gray thought Atkinson's appointment was the perfect move by Doug Ellis, as much to return some charisma and personality to a club that had lost its spark since the departure of Graham Taylor.

'Graham had a distinct way of playing,' Gray said. 'He never changed things too much, made second at Watford, which was an unbelievable achievement, then he did the same at Villa. It was going to be hard for Dr Jo to enjoy the same results with that group of players playing in a way that was very different to how Graham's teams played.

'Dr Jo had done OK. I don't think Vengloš was an absolute failure, he had done some good things. But once Big Ron seemed available, a manager with that kind of character and track record was the kind of manager and personality that Villa needed.

'Vengloš was probably a good coach but as a personality, was he what Villa needed? Probably not. He was more reserved and wasn't out there like Big Ron was. Under Big Ron, Villa soon had that spark and expectation about them again.'

1990/91 season:

League position: 17th (of 20)

League Cup: quarter-final (lost 4-1 at Leeds United)

FA Cup: third round (lost 1-0 in a replay at Wimbledon)

UEFA Cup: second round (lost 3-2 on aggregate to Inter Milan)

Top scorers: David Platt 24; Tony Cascarino 10; Derek Mountfield 6

11

Platt Says Arrivederci

'It became pretty obvious he was set on going to Bari. I could see in training that his mind was somewhere else, which was understandable.'

– Ron Atkinson

THERE WAS an inevitability about David Platt's eventual transfer from Aston Villa to Serie A that had lingered from the moment he scored his incredible winner for England against Belgium in the 1990 World Cup.

What was less sure was which Italian club he would be signing for.

'There was a lot of talk around the place ever since the World Cup that Platty was taking Italian lessons and he wouldn't be with us for long,' secretary Steve Stride said.

Although Platt finally departed in the summer of 1991, he had privately spent a whole season at Villa plotting his next career move to Italy. It never affected his form at Villa, as his 24-goal tally would testify, and he was no less committed to the cause, but the near-relegation under Jozef Vengloš crystallised the fact that he was just too good to be at Aston Villa then. Forget the fact they almost won the First Division under Graham Taylor in 1990. Clubs are ultimately only as good as their last season and the stats suggested that Villa were hanging on to their status in the top flight by a thread. Platt was always going to be away in the summer of 1991.

Before his eventual move to Bari, where Villa duo Gordon Cowans and Paul Rideout had moved in 1985, he had received all kinds of hints and innuendoes from various Italian clubs such as Genoa, Fiorentina, Sampdoria – courtesy of third-party conversations involving Liam Brady – and Inter Milan, after his goal at Villa Park against them, when their managing director indicated after the game they would be bidding for him and subsequently gave Platt an Inter pin badge to wear on his lapel. Nothing materialised from any of it, but the momentum of his move kept building.

In the meantime, as Villa's miserable season unfolded, Platt started taking Italian language lessons on Friday afternoons after training. He also improved his diet to one that involved pasta, white meat, fish and vegetables. He improved his stamina and agility through extra fitness classes with Paul Barron, away from Villa. Platt's lifestyle was all pointing to a new direction in Italy. He now just needed the long-awaited move to materialise.

Bari was not the club Platt would have chosen had he been given the choice but through the mutual relationship with Cowans, *I Galletti* exploited that angle and made a firm approach. The Italians visited Platt during the latter stages of the 1990/91 season, both officially with Doug Ellis's knowledge and blessing, and unofficially. Platt went to Bari to meet them again and look around the stadium. He was even paraded in front of the Italian media before he had agreed to sign for them. Eventually, Platt made up his mind: Bari would not be the right move for him for footballing reasons. His refusal to dive into that transfer opened other avenues as Marseille made an approach.

By this time, Ron Atkinson had started his tenure at Villa Park. Atkinson had Platt at Manchester

United as a youth player before releasing him to Crewe Alexandra, so the history wasn't good. Atkinson was an admirer of Platt as a footballer, but he quickly became exasperated by all the speculation linking him with a move away from Villa. Therefore, at the Bodymoor Heath training ground one morning, Atkinson approached Platt and said pointedly, 'Are you staying with us or are you going to Bari?' That was the nudge Platt needed because if he was being honest with himself, he had no interest in spending another season at Villa, though he was flattered by the many letters in the local newspapers from supporters urging Villa not to sell him.

'Platty was pretty close to going to Bari before I got to Villa,' Atkinson recalled. 'It was a huge blow because he was the best player there. But the plus side was that the £5m or so we were getting was a huge help towards the rebuilding of the squad.

'It became obvious he was set on going to Bari. I could see in training that his mind was somewhere else, which was understandable. At first, I was willing to keep him till maybe October and see if he changed his thinking. But eventually I said to Andy [Gray], "No, let's deal with it now, get the money and rebuild this squad!" The good thing about Doug was if he had the money, he would give it to you for players if you put up a good case for them.'

Platt's true ambition was playing in Serie A, though, and he was naturally pleased when Bari tabled further offers to him with the financial benefits increasing each time. After advice from people he respected like Bobby Robson, he eventually agreed to move to Bari, while at a pre-season training camp in Germany with Villa.

The terms of the move were renegotiated after the impasse in the transfer, taking the initial £4.5m deal to a record £5.5m, as Platt still had two years remaining on his Villa contract. Platt's agent and former Villa commercial manager Tony Stephens led the talks on the personal terms, while Ellis was heavily involved with the club finances. Steve Stride said Ellis included a 50 per cent sell-on clause and negotiated a testimonial between Villa and Bari that meant the overall transfer fee would be reduced by £500,000. That match was never played.

So, there it was. Platt was no longer an Aston Villa player and Atkinson had plenty of money to spend on reshaping his squad. Most of Platt's team-mates were disappointed to see him go, while others felt it might end up as a blessing.

'He was a massive loss,' Tony Daley commented. 'I would have loved for us to have kept him because he was a quality player, but you cannot stop a player who ripped it up from leaving as he was looking to broaden his career. He was subsequently very successful in Italy and proved that he was right to go there when he did.'

Tony Cascarino was another who greatly admired Platt's achievements for Villa, but he also felt that the team would benefit all-round once they were not set up to play only to the strengths of the goalscoring midfielder. His thinking was reminiscent of how Villa improved as a team after the loss of star player Alan McInally in 1989. Sometimes, you need to lose the key man to make the team better as a whole, which also proved to be the case when Andy Gray left in 1979.

'I felt like Villa's whole system was lined up to suit David, which certainly never helped me,' Cascarino commented. 'That's not me blaming him, as David was a fantastic finisher, with his feet or his head, he was a real confident boy in front of goal. He was quite average in lots of ways, but he had a great engine and could drive forward. He wasn't a great technical player in the way that a Trevor Francis was, but he was an effective finisher which made him successful.

'I don't want this to sound horrible, but I felt that David's heart wasn't in it in that 1990/91 season. The lads knew he was learning Italian, which is what the foreign players did when they were getting ready to move. Nobody dared to stand up to him by saying, "Oi you, never mind about going to Italy, when are you going to turn up for us?" No one said that because he was still our best player and was scoring goals.

'I don't want to be critical of David but even he himself would probably say, "I wasn't the best, but I could match the best." That's the sort of player I thought David was. He wasn't a technical genius, but he could match the best through his goalscoring numbers.'

12

Ron's Revolution – The Victims

'It was an acrimonious exit for me at Villa because Ron treated me quite mean and nasty. I accept managers have their own ideas about who they want to keep and who they want to sell but I thought Ron didn't treat me very well and I deserved more respect.'

– Derek Mountfield

RON ATKINSON arrived at Villa Park on 7 June 1991. He expected initially to take his time assessing the squad's strengths and weaknesses and slowly make a few changes, in and out. Well, that was his plan. But immediately he set about significant surgery of the playing squad and backroom staff.

His first major decision was to appoint former Holte End hero Andy Gray as his assistant. Gray was, of course, the PFA Player and Young Player of the Year in 1977 while at Villa in his first spell, and Atkinson was then based not too far away when manager of West Bromwich Albion. He saw the impact Gray had on Villa and later signed him in his second stint as Baggies boss in 1987/88. Gray's influence around the squad as a senior pro made a positive impression on Big Ron and that was fresh in his mind when he thought about who to take as his assistant in 1991.

'Peter Withe wasn't really an option as he had already taken the reserves manager job by the time I got there,' Atkinson explained. 'I made him chief scout as well. I'd had Andy with me at West Brom and I knew his thoughts on the game, and I thought, "Yeah, I'm not unhappy with that at all, we think on the same lines about the game."'

Gray was equally delighted to link up once again with Atkinson and, especially, to return to Aston Villa, a club he loved dearly having signed for them in 1975 from Dundee United.

'I was doing some work for TV but Sky Sports, as it later became, hadn't really kicked in by that stage,' Gray said. 'It was clear that the television work I was doing would not interfere with what Ron wanted me to do for him. So, I was combining both roles as I jumped at the chance to go back to Villa.'

Gray remembers those early days in training with Atkinson, who he saw assessing the players with a degree of scepticism. With Doug Ellis availing around £5m from the David Platt sale to Atkinson to reinvest in the squad, he was keen to get to work on some targets very quickly.

'Ron told me he was going to give the existing squad an opportunity to show him what they can do,' Gray revealed. 'We got the guys in a little earlier for pre-season and after about three days of training, Ron came up to me and said, "No, I'm not having this lot. Forget what I said, we need to go out and get a few otherwise we're going to get relegated."

'He felt very quickly that the group he had inherited was not going to be good enough and Ron then just went out there into the market and went bang, bang, bang, bang – I think six came in in next to no time.'

Atkinson made his mind up almost immediately that he was not going to keep record signing Tony Cascarino.

'When I was at Sheffield and we played against Millwall, I had always fancied the other lad, [Teddy]

Sheringham,' Atkinson recalled. 'Cas was the big fish at the time, but I'd tell my staff, "I prefer the number ten." Still, I didn't go into Villa with a preconceived idea of Cas. Not until we had a staff match and he played with us to try to get fit for the start of the season. He had a touch of a rhino. Afterwards he told [physio] Jim Walker, "I don't think I've done myself any favours today." To be fair to Jim, he didn't tell me that until two years later. It was nothing personal and I liked Cas as a bloke and even now I think he's very good on the radio. But back then Liam Brady did me a favour by offering to give us our money back to take him to Celtic. He surprised me, knowing the way he played, that he would fancy the type that Cas was.'

For the player, it was a sad time because he never wanted to leave Villa Park having not performed to the standard that had been expected of him when he signed.

'I had gone through my career getting thumbs-ups everywhere, whether at Gillingham or Millwall, and then I got to the Villa, and it was the first time that I felt like I had let people down,' Cascarino revealed. 'I wasn't helped that Graham Taylor left as he would have got the best out of me, I'm sure. I was a different player when I trained hard.

'I found it hard to leave Villa Park. It was probably my biggest regret leaving the Villa when I did. I really didn't want to go. I didn't have much choice about it, but I would rather have been a success there than leave when I did. The reception I got on my debut at Derby County was incredible and it's a memory that's still with me today. I always appreciated how the Villa fans kept backing me and were behind me, even though I wasn't at my best. I was used to being at Millwall where the fans hammer you and if you're not playing well, they will tell you "You're fucking shit!"

'As soon as Ron came in, though, it was clear I would be on my way. There would be no chances, he had made his mind up about me. My first conversation with Big Ron was: "Hey Tony." "Hey Ron." "We've agreed a fee with Celtic for you."

'I spoke to Southampton as well. I could have gone there. I didn't have a problem with Ron. I had a problem with leaving the Villa but not with Ron. There's a lot to be said for managers who are totally upfront with you. I scored a great goal against Ron's Sheffield Wednesday for Millwall and had an outstanding match. So, when I heard Ron was coming to the Villa, I hoped he would remember that match. But it wasn't to be. I used to be a non-league player so when I was rusty my touch could look bad, I get it.

'If you saw me play on a bad day, you'd never touch me. But when I was on my game, I could be a real handful. But fair play to Ron, he told me straight that he was going to bring big Cyrille [Regis] in.

'I didn't really want to go to the SPL but having met with Liam Brady, it felt like the right move as Celtic are a great club. But in hindsight I probably should have gone to Southampton, but because me and Liam were close that never happened.'

As is normally the case in football clubs when a new manager arrives, there are always casualties of the new regime and though Cascarino accepted his fate somewhat philosophically, not all the early departures felt so accepting of their forced exits from Villa Park. There were only four significant players that Atkinson inherited and did not sell – Bryan Small, Dwight Yorke, Paul McGrath and Nigel Spink. Tony Daley and Steve Froggatt almost survived Atkinson's reign until they moved to Wolves in 1994.

Derek Mountfield and Kevin Gage were two examples of players who believed they deserved the opportunity to prove their worth to Atkinson. Successful managers, however, must be ruthless and

Big Ron had no problem in showing the door to those players who he thought needed upgrading, even though the players felt differently.

Gage was sold to Sheffield United for £150,000. Although he ended up becoming a club legend at Bramall Lane (he was their player of the year in 1994/95) and still to this day lives and works in the area, back then it wasn't a transfer he welcomed.

'I've always been a bit upset about how my time at Villa finished,' Gage said. 'We knew early in the summer that Ron was coming in and I wanted to make a good impression on him so I came in early to get as fit as I could. I probably had the best pre-season in terms of my form that I had ever had as a footballer. I don't usually blow my own trumpet but in this one game, which was in Germany I think, I was outstanding. Ron wasn't there but I know his staff told him, but maybe he needed to see it with his own eyes.

'It soon became very clear that I was not going to be a part of his plans whatsoever. He signed all his new players that he wanted to bring in to shake up the team, and all the old guard – of which I was one – were stuck in the reserves. It was the first time that had ever happened to me because I had either been in the first team or at least on the edge of it. It really got to me, and my motivation evaporated. I went to see Atkinson as did about four or five of us like Ian Ormondroyd and Stuart Gray, and was told, "You're not part of my plans, find yourself another club." That was it. To be fair to Atkinson, I understand that he needed to make changes as the team hadn't performed well the season before and he brought in some outstanding players like [Kevin] Richardson and [Steve] Staunton, but I hoped to get a chance to prove myself to him. I didn't get that opportunity through no fault of my own.

'It got to the stage about four games into the season where there were hardly any midfield players fit and the coaching staff was telling Atkinson to play me. Instead of doing that he played Kent Nielsen in the centre of midfield and once he did that, I said to myself, "That's me completely done." That should never have happened. I thoroughly enjoyed my time at Villa and it was a shame that my days there ended on a bit of a sour note.'

Mountfield was in discussions with Villa about a new contract just as Jozef Vengloš was leaving the club. He regretted not completing business quickly because as soon as Atkinson entered the building, it became clear the defender was not going to be a part of his plans.

'I don't think Ron fancied him,' Andy Gray said. 'Derek was a good player who I played with at Everton – we won the title together. But it was unfortunate for Derek because he was never going to get in ahead of Paul [McGrath] and Ron had just brought in Shaun Teale who he liked the look of, so Derek's prospects weren't great. Especially as Shaun was a left-footer and could play on the left side of big Paul, and Ron liked that balance. The double act of Teale and McGrath was the combination that Ron fancied, and you have to say in hindsight he wasn't wrong.'

The signing of Teale was a bitter blow for Mountfield as he knew then his chance of staying on in Big Ron's new world at Villa was remote. The irony in Mountfield's sale was that Atkinson very nearly bought him for Manchester United from Tranmere Rovers a decade earlier before Everton did.

'I'd worked my bollocks off during pre-season training to get myself fit,' Mountfield recalled. 'I was flying. Then he named his squad for a tour of Germany and didn't include me. I dashed down the training ground to speak to him and he was quite abrupt with me and said, "You haven't signed your new contract so you're not coming, sod off." I trained with the kids while they were in Germany and because they struggled out there, I came back in and trained with the first team again.

'I even started the season when we won at Sheffield Wednesday, then once we lost at home to Manchester United, I wasn't in the squad for the next game. He barely spoke to me after that. It was an acrimonious exit for me at Villa because Ron treated me quite mean and nasty. I accept managers have their own ideas about who they want to keep and who they want to sell but I thought Ron didn't treat me very well and I deserved more respect. I didn't let it affect my memories of playing for the club, though, and I still love going back there. I have a lot of friends at Villa and the fans were always good to me and still are.'

Mountfield's fellow central defender Kent Nielsen was also moved on, but he would have no complaints as he went on to win the Danish Cup with new club Aarhus in 1992, the same year he also collected a winners' medal in the European Championship when Denmark shocked the football world.

'Kent was a great lad,' Atkinson said, 'a good pro, but a bit of a "Steady Eddie" and seeing as I already had young Ugo [Ehiogu] and Teale, as well as Macca, I didn't need him. The best game he had for me was against Forest when I stuck him man for man on Nigel Clough. There was an alarming lack of pace between them!' That was the match Gage referred to as being the last straw for him when he saw Nielsen selected ahead of him in midfield.

Gage and Mountfield were just two of a significant number eventually shipped out by Atkinson. Some were angry at their transfers, others accepted the news well, while others just took it in their stride as a part of football.

'Ron had carte blanche as the new manager to do what he felt he needed to do,' Stuart Gray commented. 'As captain I hoped I could stay on as one of his senior players, but he soon made it clear I wasn't a part of his plans. While it hurt, I had to accept it and move on. I wasn't 21, I was 31 so I moved on to Southampton.'

Similarly, Ian Ormondroyd was disappointed to be leaving Villa Park but appreciated the honesty from Atkinson that all managers do not always deal in.

'He came in and just said, "Sorry son, you're not for me, you're not my type of player, but I'll find you a decent club." I said, "Fair enough, Ron." At least he was honest, and he did help me get a move to Derby County. He also brought Cyrille Regis in who was class, so I could have no complaints.'

Striker Ian Olney became another victim of the Atkinson revolution. He was not an instant sale and actually made 16 starts in the 1991/92 campaign but his three goals were not enough to earn him more time to prove himself to Ron, who eventually paid for more quality and experience in the following season in the shape of Dean Saunders.

'Olney was another "Steady Eddie",' Atkinson said. 'I was a bit disappointed in him because I had high hopes for him when I went there. I certainly wasn't in a hurry to sell him, but he just didn't do it for me. It was a good deal for the club when Joe Royle came in for him and paid us £750,000 [a club record for Oldham Athletic].'

Royle maintains Olney was a terrific signing for Oldham. His return of 14 goals in 53 appearances for the Latics wasn't great but his all-round play fitted in well with the style of football that Royle played.

'When Graham Taylor had given me the under-21s job, Olney was one of the four centre-forwards I had, along with a fellow called Alan Shearer,' Royle recalled. 'I loved Olney's movement – he was very fluent as a player and he brought others into play, which was the way I liked to operate, he was my type of centre-forward. He was doing great for us until he got a terrible injury that ended his career. It was such a shame because he would have gone on to better things. He was a nice kid as well.

'In the 12 years I was there, we made a profit on transfers every year. But I had to really convince the club to release the money for Olney, as it was a lot for us to pay. We were on the up at that time, though. I still have some older fans say to me at Oldham, "It was a shame about Olney wasn't it Joe," and I always say, "It bloody was, because the kid could play!"'

Gary Penrice was one of Jozef Vengloš's three signings and he also never lasted long under Atkinson. He did feature in eight league games in August and September of 1991, even scoring his only goal for Villa in that time against Arsenal. But, ultimately, he was on borrowed time as the new manager looked for extra quality in front of goal.

'He was a decent little player,' Atkinson revealed, 'but it was that natural progression I was looking for and once I bought players like Dalian Atkinson and Cyrille in, I had got to offload a few at the same time. You had to wheel and deal in those days.'

Chris Price played just four games in five months under Atkinson and his last match came in a 2-1 defeat at Carrow Road in January 1992 when he was used as an emergency left-back, with new signing Dariusz Kubicki taking his old place at right-back. Price was sold back to his former club Blackburn Rovers for £90,000 and played a bit-part in helping them regain promotion to the top flight. After a 4-1 home defeat to Leeds United in November 1991, Villa legend Gordon Cowans made the same move to Ewood Park, for £175,000, though he was to return for a third spell at his beloved club.

'Sid was slightly different, slightly older from the Sid I knew at Villa years before,' said Andy Gray, who still saw the quality of the player, nonetheless, as Cowans played 15 matches right from the beginning of Atkinson's tenure before the Blackburn switch.

'None of us move around the pitch as well as we could when we were ten years younger, but the mobility he had lost in that time was more than compensated by his quality and experience. You never lose your touch.

'Gordon Cowans was one of the best one-touch passers of a football I ever saw in my life, left or right foot. The ball would come to him and it would be dispatched 50 yards or so first time and more often than not be right on the money. He probably didn't score enough goals in his career for the talent he had.

He was such a beautiful striker of the ball that I would have loved to see Sid get 12 goals a season because he was that good.

'But at this time, later on in his career, he was still well worth his place in the squad and more than anything, he was the right kind of character we wanted. You want good personalities and good pros in your dressing room, players who still wanted to do it and win games and you could never question Sid for his attitude.'

Winger Nigel Callaghan was loaned out to former club Watford and Huddersfield Town, but he was unable to find another permanent club and ended up at non-league Stafford Rangers, the town where he settled to live. Callaghan was asked for an interview for this book but commented, 'No thank you, I don't have a good word to say about my time at the Villa.'

So why was Callaghan so bitter about his three years at Villa Park, even more than 30 years later? Well, during the Covid-19 lockdown, he published a podcast that highlighted bullying claims against Villa's management.

Atkinson commented, 'I knew Cally when he was at Watford. He scored the winning goal in a cup match against us at Man United. But by the time I got to Villa, he was a minimum two stone overweight. I didn't recognise him at first. I put him on a fitness regime and asked Peter Withe to look after him. He had to get into the training ground at 9am and do a session with the team and then another one in the afternoon with Peter. Either Peter or Jim Walker gave him a bike to cycle home to Tamworth and into training in the morning, but someone found it propped up against a lamp-post down the road. He had completely gone. He went out on loan but ended up in non-league and I'm surprised he played at that level given his lack of fitness. He hadn't got a prayer.'

13

Magic Macca, and How He Almost Left the Villa

'By the time I reached the Villa, the Macca boozing stories concerned me and I thought, "I might have to get rid of this problem."'

– Ron Atkinson

A KNOCK on Ron Atkinson's office door at the training ground from Gordon Cowans led to one of the most significant decisions in Aston Villa's history. That, and the adulation of thousands of Villa supporters for Paul McGrath.

Atkinson was still finding his feet as the Villa boss and having managed the brilliant but wayward genius that was McGrath at Manchester United for three years before, he was asking himself if he should tolerate the off-field antics that went with him, namely his penchant for alcohol. Big Ron was the man who brought McGrath to England when he paid Irish club St Patrick's £30,000 for him in 1983. At that time, he had the chance to sign either Derek Mountfield from Tranmere Rovers, Mark Wright from Oxford United, or McGrath. He took the Irish lad and never regretted it. To this day Atkinson regards that piece of business as the shrewdest pound-for-pound deal he ever made as a manager. The best player he signed, he says, was Bryan Robson for £1.5m. But the best value was McGrath.

When the disciplinarian Alex Ferguson came in to succeed Atkinson at United, he was shocked to discover the extent of the drinking antics going on after training and McGrath was identified as a culprit along with club captain Bryan Robson and Norman Whiteside, among others. Ferguson had no intention of selling Robson so to disband the group he eventually sold McGrath to Villa and Whiteside to Everton.

When Atkinson inherited McGrath he knew he was lucky to have a player of his calibre but wondered if the downside outweighed the benefits.

Atkinson was back in Birmingham wheeling and dealing to improve his squad when the players flew out to Germany for a pre-season tour in 1991. Andy Gray was left in charge as Ron's number two, and he soon realised how stressful management could be off the field as well as on it.

'Everyone at the club or everyone who knew Macca knew he had a problem,' Gray said. 'Playing-wise it never affected him. But every now and again he would have a wobble. Jim Walker handled him better than anyone and was a calming influence on Paul. I saw it first-hand very early on in my time as a coach at Villa when Paul went AWOL in Germany, after he had climbed out of his hotel room window to go into town. Jim seemed quite relaxed, while I was fretting. We went out looking for him and found him in a little bar. He was as good as gold and was full of apologies saying, "Please don't tell the gaffer." We didn't want to make Paul feel bad about it and made out that we bumped into him by accident.'

Atkinson said such a story was not a one-off; there were many similar tales around McGrath.

'At one stage early on in my time at Villa, it looked like I was signing a player a day,' said Atkinson. 'Andy [Gray] took the boys to Ireland for a warm-up match while I was due to fly out later for the game. Andy rang me and said, "Gaffer, there's a problem. The big man has gone missing." Once Macca got to Ireland, he was treated like royalty, so we had to keep him close at all times, under lock and key almost. By the time I got there he'd turned up and Andy said, "You can't play him." I said, "We're in Ireland, so not only is he playing, but he's captain!"

'We kicked off and it soon became obvious Paul was still pissed. We had a free kick, Sid went to take it before Paul pushed him out of the way and said he'd take it. He ran up to the ball and took an air shot! I'd seen enough and shouted, "Sid, tell Paul his ankle is hurting and he's coming off."'

The Villa job meant the world to Atkinson and he was concerned that this troubled defender might become a huge problem for him.

A chance enquiry from McGrath's former Republic of Ireland team-mate Liam Brady, who was now manager of Celtic, presented Big Ron with something of a dilemma. Here was his opportunity to offload the player who gave him the biggest headache when the players were left to their own devices. The other side of his quandary was that McGrath was his best player.

'The stories I was hearing about McGrath was not the McGrath I had left at Manchester United,'

Atkinson revealed. 'All the drink stories surprised me because, while I knew he liked the pop, he never missed a day's training for me there. I think what happened, after I left United, Macca got injured and they put him and Norman together working the lounges on matchdays as they both had long-term injuries and it was a way of getting them to earn their money. They were two phenomenal players. But all that time together might not have been such a good idea because I understand they enjoyed the club hospitality a little bit too much.

'So, by the time I reached the Villa the Macca boozing stories concerned me and I thought, "I might have to get rid of this problem." I spoke to Liam Brady and he was going to take him. Liam offered £750,000. I said, "No, if he's going it has to be £1.5m." If they'd come up with the money, I think we would have sold him because I just thought I didn't need this problem in a new job at the Villa.

'It was a lucky escape because he played at Sheffield Wednesday in my first game at right-back and he was brilliant, and I soon put him back into the middle. I had a right touch of good fortune there!'

Brady remembers things a little differently, but the overriding conclusion is the same, which is that

Atkinson opted not to sell McGrath in the event, but he sure came close.

'The way I understand it is that I offered the £750,000 initially and Ron told me he would sell him, but the fee had to be £1.2m. I agreed and we did eventually come back with the money but by then I think Paul had played a game or two more and was the best man on the park in both games. Ron then turned round to me and said, "If I sell him now the Villa fans will slaughter me and burn the place down," so it never happened. It worked out well for Paul and Villa, but it was a shame for Celtic because Paul was a fantastic defender.'

Back to that knock on the door from Gordon Cowans. Atkinson well remembered the conversation he had with Cowans about the importance of McGrath to Villa. The message struck a chord with the manager given the normally quiet nature of Cowans and how he took it upon himself to make sure Atkinson fully understood the players' views on the subject, even though he was not even speaking as the club captain, just someone who wanted the best for Villa.

'The players must have heard about this Macca to Celtic story,' Big Ron recalled, 'because Sid came to see me and said, "Gaffer, don't worry about the drinking stories, the players absolutely love Macca. Don't sell him." That meant a lot to me because one thing I was concerned about was if I made allowances for Macca's drinking, how many other players would think they can get away with the same behaviour? I didn't want that issue to worry about. Pretty soon, it all settled down and I realised how important Paul was for us. But that conversation with Sid was quite significant and it made me feel a lot better about keeping him.'

Atkinson grew to accept McGrath's personal life was how it was and relied on his physio Jim Walker to manage things as best he could, which he did excellently, even travelling to international matches with him to ensure he was not able to get up to mischief while alone. The whole squad was understanding of McGrath's lifestyle and appreciated him for what he was rather than what he might be.

Andy Gray: 'Paul was one of the best players I ever came up against. I knew he was a terrific footballer from my playing days but it's only when you start working with these guys you realise just *how good* he was. He was a sensational footballer, a great lad, had his problems, he had to cope with them, and he did as well as he could while being a professional footballer.

The level of his performances week in and week out was quite extraordinary.

'It was incredible how Macca didn't train all week, but Ron knew how to treat him to get the best out of him. Paul would come jogging out on a Monday morning for training and Ron would say, "Macca, go and relax in the bath." Same Tuesday, we'd give him Wednesday off, Thursday, "Macca have a bath", Friday, "we're practising free kicks and corners so stay out for that", then Saturday he'd be the best player on the pitch. He was amazing, a great lad, shy, a team player and he loved his football.

'Ron knew what a talent he was, and the boys didn't have a problem with the special treatment he got because he was Macca, a one-off.

'Even when all the new players came in, within a month they knew what kind of a talent they were playing with in Paul. If he missed a game on a Saturday, we were always poorer for his absence. He was as quick as anyone, he could read the game better than anyone, though he was hopeless at playing the offside trap, always ten yards deeper than he should have been, but that was Paul. Nobody enjoyed playing against him.'

Tony Cascarino: 'I knew Paul really well, he was a quiet man but he was wild and there was a lot going on around him. His private life was on another level. Graham Taylor asked me to room with Paul on away trips as he wanted Paul to be with someone he knew from the Republic of Ireland team. I could tell so many stories about him that don't reflect particularly well on Paul, but I won't because everyone loved him. Without a drink he's the nicest man in the world. With a drink he could be an animal, a beast, depending on how many he had of course.

'I knew what to expect as everyone in the Ireland team protected Paul and that was the same scenario at the Villa. I wouldn't say he was like a child, but he needed care and protection to stop him from going off the rails.

'What went in Paul's favour, of course, and why he got so much latitude if you like from team-mates and managers, is that he was outstanding in nearly every game he played.'

Kevin Richardson: 'All the boys knew about his issues, but he just used to come into training and go off with Jim Walker and do his own thing, like weights, or the bike to keep himself ticking over. Later, he lived in Manchester and his wife would bring him into training and drop him off, and he would do his thing. I don't know how he got back home, if he got back home. I would just hear little bits from the sidelines and didn't really want to know any more.

'I felt we just had to let the fella live his life the way he wanted to live it as it's not like whatever he was doing was really affecting his performances as he was always getting man of the match. I used to think I'm not sure if he's on any medication but if he is, I want some of it! He was incredible. His reading of the game was on another level and made up for a few of his shortcomings. Shaun Teale also combined well with Paul and would have helped him out on many occasions. They were a good pairing.'

Stuart Gray: 'We were aware of his problems and that's where Jim Walker played a huge part in being a mentor for him. Macca didn't train much but come the weekend he would usually be our best player. His problems off the pitch were well documented but ultimately what motivated him was Saturday afternoon, not Friday in the gym, but in a match when it mattered. I have lost count of the amount of times Macca back-heeled a ball off the goal line or a cleared dangerous ball over the top of our defence.'

Ian Ormondroyd: 'He was class. Most people who played with him say he was the best player they ever played with – that's certainly my verdict. David

Platt was very good, scoring goals, box-to-box, but Paul McGrath was the best player every week, despite his problems with his knees and off the field. Such a lovely quiet guy as well.'

Tony Daley: 'There was a weekly comedy sketch between Macca and the physio Jim Walker. After a match on Saturday, Jim would ask, "Paul, how are you feeling?" He would say, "I've got no chance for Wednesday, Jim." Then he would come in on the Monday hobbling around, have some treatment, as he didn't train, still saying he's got no chance of playing. By Wednesday morning, Macca would say, "I'm feeling a bit better, Jim, but I'm struggling for tonight." But after more treatment he would end up playing and be man of the match. That exchange seemed to happen every week!'

14

The New Faces of Ron's Revolution

'With Ron, he liked good players obviously but what was equally important for him was having good characters in the dressing room and players who would be leaders on the field.'

– Kevin Richardson

ONCE RON Atkinson decided he was not having much of the squad he inherited from Graham Taylor and then Jozef Vengloš, the transfer comings and goings were volatile. It wasn't enjoyable for those players being asked to find a new club, but for the supporters and those players on their way in, there was a distinct buzz of excitement around Villa Park as expectations soared, quickly.

'It was obvious Ron had quickly identified the weaknesses in the squad and been given the go-ahead by the chairman to spend some money because he was very busy in the transfer market straight away,' said Kevin Richardson, Atkinson's first captain and one of his earliest signings.

Atkinson almost raided his former club Sheffield Wednesday immediately for central defender Nigel Pearson. He knew he was going to offload Kent Nielsen and Derek Mountfield, hadn't yet signed up Ugo Ehiogu or Shaun Teale, and was identifying talent to play alongside Paul McGrath.

'Nigel's contract was up, and I had spoken to him about Villa when I knew I was going there,' Big Ron recalled. 'I think deep down he wanted to stay at Wednesday. So, I said to the chairman Dave Richards, "You've got 24 hours to sort his contract out, and if you don't, I'll bring him to Villa." They signed him to a new contract almost immediately.

'I kind of knew that would happen but while I would happily have signed him, it was my way of looking after the player. If I'd have signed Pearson, there would probably have been no Teale signing.'

The player merry-go-round was instant and the fans were ready to savour the ride. There was nothing more exciting than a player transfer story adorning the back page of the *Birmingham Evening Mail* newspaper and Atkinson kept the local journalists very busy in that regard.

'With Ron, he liked good players obviously but what was equally important for him was having good characters in the dressing room and players who would be leaders on the field,' Richardson said. 'I would have been one such player who wasn't afraid to say to my team-mates, "Pull your socks up, you're better than that!" But maybe I wouldn't be as polite!

'Andy Gray knew my temperament; he knew I was a shouter who always demanded a lot from my team-mates. Andy would have told Ron that I would sort the boys out on the field.

'All those new players who came in were hungry to win things and the boys who were already there got a grasp of our mentality and we all had a real go, at the league especially.'

Richardson had his former Everton team-mate Gray to thank for being signed at Villa, as Atkinson was only a casual admirer. Gray and Richardson shared a dressing room at Goodison Park when Howard Kendall's highly successful team won the First Division, the FA Cup and the Cup Winners' Cup.

'I like to think I was responsible for bringing Richo into Villa,' Gray admitted. 'I floated his name and Ron then asked me about him and I said, "Go get him. He's there every day, every game with great qualities and might not be flashy but you know what you're going to get from him every week." Once Richo was through the door, Ron said to me some time later that he never realised Richo was as good as he was. I had played with him at Everton and knew all about him. He won the title at Everton, he won the title at Arsenal, and nearly won it at Villa. You don't do that if you're not a good player.'

Richardson ended up as an ever-present in his first season, playing 42 league games in 1991/92. He was grateful that his old mate persuaded Atkinson to sign him. Atkinson appreciated Richardson so much in the event he not only made him captain but signed him again for Coventry City, three years later.

'Andy kept badgering Ron to sign me, and I can't thank Andy enough for his faith in me because I had a great time at Villa,' Richardson added.

'I was obviously aware that they had won the European Cup and had a good reputation for going far in cup competitions. And it felt like only a matter of time before they went the whole hog and won the league again or won another cup. There was something building there, and I was happy to be a part of it. I liked the partnership that Big Ron and Andy had, they never gave up. Ron wanted me to play as a holding midfielder to give the team a bit of shape and balance for when the lads were all attacking and that suited me.'

Richardson arrived from Spanish outfit Real Sociedad with striker Dalian Atkinson, who Big Ron had managed previously at Sheffield Wednesday. Richardson felt the striker was a great signing for Villa, having seen his qualities at close hand in La Liga.

'I was used to sitting back and playing on the counter, and we used to try to hit teams on the break with Dalian's pace and power,' Richo said. 'Dalian combined well with John Aldridge. Aldo had already been there a year when we went out, but the Spanish didn't know much about Dalian. They used to call him "the Black Squid" because he was dead quick, and it appeared like he had lots of legs.

'When we came up against the big boys like Barcelona and Real Madrid, Dalian was dead keen to have a right go against them. Their defenders were scared of him; they took turns in giving him a kick or a dig to try and get him injured. They couldn't do it. I have a feeling Real Madrid were interested in him at the end of the season so fair play to Ron for getting in ahead. John Aldridge was getting on a bit but his understanding with Dalian was different class in Spain. They were great together.'

There was an uneasy relationship between Gray and Dalian Atkinson as the assistant manager felt the striker was lazy. Gray once tried to motivate him when he was coming back from an injury by saying, 'Come on Dalian, you'll never get back in the team if you don't impress the gaffer.' But the striker just shrugged nonchalantly and said, 'If he doesn't pick me, I'll just get a transfer to another club where the gaffer will pick me.' Gray hated that kind of attitude. Fortunately for Dalian, the manager was more tolerant. He had been an admirer since his Ipswich Town days when he had tried to sign him, unsuccessfully, for West Brom in his second stint as manager there.

Ron Atkinson considered signing Aldridge too, to keep the strike partnership with Dalian together, but eventually ruled him out as the former Liverpool man was nearing his 33rd birthday. Atkinson later regretted not making the move as it wouldn't have cost him anything in terms of a transfer fee and Aldridge's prolific scoring form in a division lower at Tranmere Rovers demonstrated he had not lost his goal touch.

Another reason Big Ron overlooked Aldridge was that he already had his sights on signing a different experienced goalscorer, Cyrille Regis, one of his favourite strikers and a former pro he loved working with a decade earlier at West Bromwich Albion.

Regis was 33 by then and was available on a free transfer from Coventry City, where he had spent seven years and helped them win the FA Cup in 1987, the best day in the club's history, which secured Regis lifelong hero-worship from the Sky Blues supporters.

'I missed him initially at Man United because I went back to West Brom for Robbo and Remi [Moses] and was a little uneasy about taking Cyrille as well,' Atkinson revealed. 'I don't think they would have sold him then anyway otherwise the fans would have torn the place down. Moving on a few years, we had Alan Brazil at United, and I was told we had to get him out the building sharp because his back was going to go in the next 12 months, which it did. I had seen Cyrille play for Coventry and thought he was easily their best player. But I still didn't move for him then.

'But when I got to Villa, I felt we were light up front with Cascarino leaving and Yorke wasn't quite ready. I felt Cyrille would be great on a free and give us a bit of presence up front and buy us a year before we could make a move for someone younger, as it proved. He was fabulous in the dressing room with his professionalism and set the perfect example I was looking for from one of my senior players – as I knew he would.

'I have been lucky over the years to have lots of good senior pros in my squads like Robbo, Cyrille, Richo and plenty of others. I always treated them with respect and as adults and let them have a drink, but they needed to know when to knuckle down. I always said, "Have a drink, enjoy yourself, but don't go too far. If you do and the police get involved, you're on your own. The club won't be there to help you. See you at training at 10am."

'I never had to worry about that stuff with Cyrille.'

Atkinson eventually signed the central defender he had wanted, having missed Nigel Pearson. Ron's ally Jim Barron had scouted Bournemouth stopper Shaun Teale for Everton so he was aware of him, but the transfer only happened after Cherries manager Harry Redknapp called Atkinson.

'He said, "Ron, I've got a player here who would be great for you, and I'll let you have him for less than what he's worth because we're desperate for the money." We checked him out and paid about £250,000 I think it was,' Atkinson recalled. 'We were ready to sell Derek Mountfield, so the timing was right. It wasn't much of a gamble and the fact he was left-sided worked well for us. He did very well for us. I mostly trusted Harry's word, but I had noticed him a year earlier when I went to St Andrew's to watch Jamie [Redknapp] and I thought then the centre-back is all right. But I was looking at Jamie at that time. It was a convenient deal for everyone. I used to get on well with Harry, still do, and he knew that I would be on the lookout for players having just gone in at Villa.

'I then had Teale, Macca and Kent Nielsen and signed Ugo as a prospect just after, while Mountfield was on his way out. I was ready to play whoever showed up best in training. Macca and one of Teale or Nielsen. Macca could play on the left side of defence, but I always felt he was better on the right side as he was predominantly a right-footed player. Teale was just strengthening the squad, but I was prepared to give him the nod if he trained well, which he did.'

The less-famous Paul Mortimer arrived from Charlton Athletic for £450,000. It wasn't a signing that lit up the Holte End, but sometimes the best signings are those who are not too well known, as John McGinn has shown in recent times. Mortimer, though, was one of Atkinson's less successful signings.

'I needed a left-sided midfielder and my contact at Charlton, Colin Clarke, who played with me at Oxford and later looked after our youth team, recommended Mortimer, though he did say he could be a bit sulky,' said Big Ron. 'Anyway, we signed him, and, after a tough start, he scored in a 4-0 win at home to Luton and then started gesturing angrily towards the Holte End. He'd got no chance once he lost the fans. I had Steve Coppell call me about him before that match so I told him if he paid us what we spent he could sign him [for Crystal Palace]. I even managed to make 50 grand on top.'

The new faces kept coming, in the 1991/92 campaign and beyond. Here are Atkinson's snapshot reasons for some of the signings (details on Ray Houghton, Dean Saunders, Steve Staunton, Ugo Ehiogu, Mark Bosnich and Andy Townsend feature in later chapters):

Poland right-back **Dariusz Kubicki** was signed while the squad was on pre-season in Germany.

Big Ron: 'We knew he had been the Poland captain and had played in the 1986 World Cup. He did OK for us, was a "Steady Eddie". There wasn't much money involved. Earl Barrett eventually replaced Dariusz. He was a good lad and managed to have a decent career at Sunderland and Wolves after he left us.'

Earl Barrett was signed in February 1992 for £1.7m from Oldham Athletic and his arrival significantly curtailed Kubicki's opportunities. The Pole was sent off in an FA Cup match at Derby County in the 1991/92 campaign and then didn't play another league game for over 18 months, as Atkinson liked Barrett to operate at right-back and not in the centre of defence where he had played so well for Oldham.

Big Ron: 'We had enough centre-halves, but I knew he could also play right-back, which was where I saw him fitting in for us. I'd seen a lot of him over the years as a kid at Man City and then at Oldham. He had always impressed me as a very quick defender. He wasn't the greatest in the attacking half of the field, but I used to say to him, "He's a good player, give it to him," if Ray Houghton, Garry Parker or those kinds of players were ahead of him.'

Joe Royle managed Barrett at Oldham and had been the one who gave him a chance after failing to make the breakthrough at Maine Road. He said of Barrett, 'He wasn't a right-back, he wasn't a centre-back, he was a defender. That was it. He wasn't Paul McGrath on the ball, but he never lost a race and he never lost a header. He wasn't great on the ball, but he wasn't bad on the ball either. The fans quickly cottoned on to him as they would chant "You'll never beat Earl Barrett". Besides that, he was a great kid. I paid just 30 grand for him from Man City, where he wasn't getting a chance, and I later sold him for £1.7m.

'I didn't want to do the deal, but we had to sell. I bought him back when I was Everton manager. That's a measure of how much I rated him. I thought the world of him and still do. I even gave him a reference for his coaching work in the US.'

Irish midfielder **Alan McLoughlin** never played a game at Villa despite signing on loan from Southampton.

Big Ron: 'I knew him as a kid at United and thought I'd have a look at him, but it didn't work out.'

Garry Parker arrived in a £650,000 move from Nottingham Forest, stayed for four years into the Brian Little tenure and played 119 matches in all competitions.

Big Ron: 'Garry was a good player and, to start with, I brought him in to play in that left-hand position where I had hoped Paul Mortimer would play. He was right-footed and better in the middle, but I looked at him as an inverted winger. Ideally, I would always have had two flying machines out wide, but if you haven't got them the next best thing for me was inverted wingers. What I mean by that is a clever player who draws people into the game and can thread through-balls to our forwards. I had seen Garry do that for Forest.'

Manchester United goalkeeper **Les Sealey** was another summer signing in July 1991, brought in on a free transfer to act as cover for Nigel Spink. Although he displaced Spink temporarily for the 1991/92 campaign, he was later demoted as reserve to Spink and subsequently returned to United on a free 18 months after he arrived.

Big Ron: 'Lee Butler went to Barnsley so Les came in as cover for Spinky. We played against him in the cup final, he was available and was a right character and I never minded characters. I'd seen David James playing for Watford when I was still at Sheffield Wednesday and I was very impressed with him. Then we watched a bit more of him and Jimmy Barron had scouted him for Everton. But as I looked at him more, I started to have doubts about him. Then out of the blue, the Bosnich move happened.'

Striker **Stefan Beinlich** and midfielder **Matthias Breitkreutz** joined on nominal fees from former East Germany club SG Bergmann-Borsig. Breitkreutz started in just ten games in three seasons while Beinlich started in seven over the same period. Beinlich was just 19 when Villa signed him and Breitkreutz was 20. Beinlich ended up winning five caps for Germany while he was at Bayer Leverkusen, where he narrowly missed out on a Bundesliga winners' medal.

Big Ron: 'I thought Breitkreutz was the better player, and his passing could be phenomenal on his day, while Beinlich was a second striker. They were two East Germans who were worth the gamble as we didn't pay much money, but, ultimately, they didn't work out and were mostly reserve team players for us.'

Midfielder **Trevor Berry** was signed for £35,000 from Bournemouth but never played a single first-team match, although he later went on to have a successful career with Rotherham United.

Dave Farrell came in from local non-league club Redditch United. He made ten appearances in more than three years, but ultimately never worked out at Villa and eventually ended up with Peterborough United, where he played over 300 games.

Big Ron: 'Farrell was lightning quick with two good feet. He never had the greatest football brain but was a flying machine. At the time we were loaded with pace. We had Tony Daley, Dalian was quick, Barrett was quick, and McGrath was quick, even though he doesn't get enough credit for that side of his game.'

Striker **Guy Whittingham** arrived from Portsmouth in August 1993 but stayed for just over a year. Midfielder **Mark Blake** went the other way as part of the deal.

Big Ron: 'He'd [Whittingham] scored a lot of goals at Portsmouth. I was happy with him, he was a good pro. He weighed in with one or two goals and it was tough on him as he was always understudy to Dalian and Deano.'

Atkinson's squad shake-up and influx of added quality was evident to Dwight Yorke, who was then still very much a youngster trying to adapt to English football and life in general.

'He offloaded the more traditional players like Ormondroyd, Olney, Mountfield and others and brought in the likes of Dalian Atkinson, who had a big rep from Real Sociedad, a proven goalscorer in Dean Saunders, a serial winner like Kevin Richardson, Garry Parker creating in midfield, the Irish contingent of Steve Staunton, Ray Houghton and later on, Andy Townsend,' Yorke said.

'That Irish contingent was very good for Villa as they had all been at good clubs and knew how to win. It didn't help the drinking culture but was still good for Villa [laughs]. So, Ron went for a bit more flamboyance and players with bigger reputations who he didn't have to wait for in terms of what they had to deliver. The youngsters were coming through like Steve Froggatt, Mark Bosnich, Ugo Ehiogu and myself, so things were looking up.'

Tony Daley was now a senior player under Atkinson and he appreciated the added quality that came in even though it limited his own first-team opportunities. He was able to see the bigger picture, as much from a supporter's viewpoint as a player's.

'There was a terrific balance throughout the squad,' Daley acknowledged. 'The senior players were like Ron's policemen on the field. As soon as that whistle went, the likes of Ray Houghton, Steve Staunton, Cyrille Regis and Kevin Richardson would all be barking at me and the others, making sure we were doing our jobs. They ran the team and that's how Ron liked it. There was no looking across to the bench for guidance as it was out there on the field.

'Add the likes of Nigel Spink and Paul McGrath who were already there, and Andy Townsend and Dean Saunders who came later, it really was a special group of players. All these guys were top professionals, but not only that, top people.

'I was never an automatic pick in the team under Ron but that showed how he improved competitiveness for the shirt. I had the likes of Ray Houghton, Dwight Yorke and Steve Froggatt to compete with.'

15

Shearer on the Radar

Atkinson was searching for a striker who would bring with him the goals that could elevate Villa towards the top of the league given he had already formed the basis of a solid defence and midfield.

'THE THING I remember most about Ron's tenure is the quality of player he was able to bring to Villa,' secretary Steve Stride lauded. 'Players I never thought we'd be able to get like Steve Staunton, Dean Saunders, Kevin Richardson. The fact we could attract this level of player and the attractive football we were playing on the pitch – it was a very positive period for the Villa.'

That's the USP that Ron Atkinson brought to Aston Villa. The man with the swagger who had walked the touchline of Old Trafford for five years had the belief he could persuade the best of players to sign for his club. He didn't always capture his targets but, nonetheless, he had the ambition to go after players that many grounded supporters would not have expected to have even been linked with their club.

Less than a year into his work at Villa, Atkinson was searching for a striker who would bring with him the goals that could elevate the team towards the top of the league given he had already formed the basis of a solid defence and midfield. In attack, he had the skills of Dalian Atkinson, but his trusted number nine Cyrille Regis was approaching the end, certainly as far as the top flight went, anyway. Dwight Yorke was on the fringes but at that time was still raw and had mostly played out wide.

Villa had sold David Platt, Tony Cascarino and Gary Penrice and had therefore raised around £6.5m and had cash to spend on new players. Atkinson looked at the Dutch striker Hans Gillhaus, who Aberdeen had signed for £650,000 from PSV Eindhoven three years earlier. He had good pedigree, but the player decided he did not want to move to Villa, who didn't go as far as making an offer anyway.

When the Gillhaus move failed to materialise, Atkinson turned briefly to a former West Ham United favourite, the Scottish striker Frank McAvennie, as a stop-gap on a short-term loan. He was not that much younger than Regis, but the manager hoped his experience would provide some goal power and know-how.

'Frank worked his socks off to try to get back to where he was at West Ham,' Atkinson said. 'He put in extra training stints, he put in everything possible. He wasn't going to cost us anything and potentially it looked a good deal, but it didn't work out in the end.'

Before the McAvennie loan earlier in 1992, Atkinson and Gray were tireless in their pursuit to strengthen the team and add more quality. They discussed a great many targets. Some were especially impressive in terms of what they ended up achieving in their careers, just not at Villa.

'Ron sent me to watch Dean Holdsworth down at Wimbledon and he was decent,' Andy Gray recalled. 'But as a counter-suggestion I said we should also consider big Duncan Ferguson up at Dundee United. I thought Ron would like him, and he did. But for some reason I'm not sure of, we didn't go for him, whether it was because we couldn't afford him or whether he was always nailed on for Rangers, I'm not sure. If we could have got him, the Villa fans would have loved him, just like the Everton fans did years later. They still talk about him at Goodison now, even though he didn't win anything.'

Atkinson admitted that he did go as far as scouting Ferguson, who had shades of Andy Gray about him with his allegiance to Dundee United, his aerial competence, his aggression, competitiveness, and his goals.

'I went up to Scotland to watch him,' said Big Ron. 'He was decent. There was a guy there who worked for *The Sun*, though I can't place his name. I was there in full disguise trying to be discreet and he walked past me and said, "Hiya Ron." I thought, "Shit, it's going to be in the papers now!" He certainly would have interested me but when we got close, we switched our attention to Dean Saunders.'

Gray referenced enquiries about Alan Shearer, too, which he felt showed Atkinson's ambition to take the club forward as much as Villa's lack of financial muscle then.

'It's really interesting that Alan Shearer was on the radar around that time,' said Gray. 'Ron liked what he saw in Shearer at Southampton and would have had him in a heartbeat.

'It soon became clear, though, that we were never going to be able to compete for him against Jack Walker's millions. As we now know, Jack soon became the king, the big money man in the league and it wasn't long before Blackburn won the league and Shearer's qualities were there for all to see.'

Atkinson added, 'Alan Shearer was the one we were keen on the most at that time. But it didn't last long because it soon became obvious that we weren't ready for him. We never got as far as speaking to Southampton. We all thought he was stitched on for United and even though we made enquiries, the consensus from those in the know was that we were wasting our time. In the event, he obviously went to Blackburn, but we couldn't have competed with Jack Walker's millions anyway.'

The discussions between Atkinson and Gray were fascinating because both were opinionated and as forthright as the other. But what was most clear was that they were only interested in what was best for Aston Villa – there would not have been too many who cared for the club as much as these two.

Gray, for instance, would routinely complain to the manager about Dalian Atkinson's lack of work rate. Gray was an all-action, bustling, battling centre-forward. He found it difficult to tolerate a striker he did not see making runs, working back, or tackling as a main part of his role. Atkinson, though, could appreciate the quality and make allowances for the player.

This background provided an interesting precursor as to how Matt Le Tissier never moved to Aston Villa when Atkinson was a huge admirer. It's not a given that the playmaker would have agreed to sign for Villa, but Atkinson was willing to make a move.

Atkinson recalled, 'Once we knew we weren't getting Shearer, I thought let's go for his mate, Le Tissier. But Andy went berserk and said, "We don't want that lazy so and so." I told Andy to get his Rothmans out and he'd find out how many goals and assists he had clocked up. I said, "Andy, we've got enough players who can run about, this is the icing on the cake signing." Anyway, I didn't let Andy put me off and I thought I had got the deal done on about three occasions but their manager Ian Branfoot, who didn't really appreciate him and wanted "dogs of war" type players, kept turning us down. I think we were bidding around the £2m mark.

'Sometimes you don't want lazy players when they don't contribute enough. But other times you'd think, "Go on, we'll tolerate him because he's a match-winner," which Dalian and Le Tissier were. Dalian was worth his weight in gold in the League Cup run in '94. Those two goals he scored in the semi-finals repaid the fee we paid for him.

'I never minded so-called lazy players and was prepared to give them a chance, as long as they gave me the creativity or goals I was looking for. I fell out with Peter Barnes at United, but he was on the verge of an England recall at the time, and I would have put him ahead of John Barnes and Chris Waddle then, after he couldn't make it work at Coventry. But he did his hamstring. You had to work with players sometimes and accept their shortcomings if they could give you that X-factor. Dalian did that for us at Villa.'

Dean Saunders soon became the big fish striker that Atkinson had been seeking. His subsequent goals would justify the £2.3m fee.

There was a buzz about Villa Park and expectation levels rose accordingly, as Atkinson continually scoured the transfer market for more quality. The added excitement was even felt in the dressing room.

'Big Ron assembled a team full of quality, experience and youth,' Tony Daley said. 'It was an exciting time to be a Villa player.'

16

Season of Promise

'Do I regret not staying and becoming the manager of Aston Villa further down the line? Sometimes, yes. Do I regret not staying on with Ron? Sometimes. We finished second the season after I left and maybe if I had stayed on, we might have won it.'

– Andy Gray

VILLA FINISHED seventh in Ron Atkinson's first campaign as manager and that certainly represented significant progress from the near relegation the season before under Jozef Vengloš.

The signs looked good immediately when Atkinson had to return to his former club Sheffield Wednesday for the first game of the season and came away with a 3-2 win. The atmosphere was hostile as the home supporters vented their anger towards Atkinson for walking out on the Owls after he indicated he would stay on.

Villa fielded six new players in their starting XI and three of them scored on their debuts, Cyrille Regis, Dalian Atkinson and Steve Staunton, while Shaun Teale, Kevin Richardson and Paul Mortimer also played that day. It was a fairy-tale result for Villa and the new manager having trailed 2-0.

'That game really stands out in my mind,' Andy Gray recalled. 'How's that for the computer throwing up such a storyline after Ron had walked out on them that summer? Ron was getting absolute pelters in the lead-up to the game and I told him, "Hey, I'm not sitting beside you on Saturday. You're on your own!"

'It was an unbelievable atmosphere, the fans and both sets of players were really up for it. The Wednesday players were desperate to beat Big Ron, but we managed to come back from two down. We were buzzing in the dressing room. I'll never forget that game, it was sensational.'

The signing of Regis was looked on with some scepticism by certain sections of the Villa fanbase because they felt their local rivals West Brom and then Coventry had had the best out of him and he was just picking up a last big pay cheque at Villa. However, from that first goal at Hillsborough through to his last day at Villa, he won over the entire support and playing squad with his commitment, work rate and professionalism.

Dwight Yorke, the surprise top scorer for Villa that season with 17 goals, said he learned so many lessons from Regis that helped prepare him for the rest of his career.

'I learned a lot from the late and great Big C [Regis],' Yorke admitted. 'He was a big part of my development. He was such a respected guy in the dressing room and was powerful and did things right on and off the field.

'The one piece of advice from Cyrille that stuck with me more than any other was when he told me, "You're great in training but you need to take that same arrogance and attitude from when you're destroying us in training into games." That stuck with me. When I eventually got to the top of the pecking order at Villa, it was because of Cyrille's advice. He encouraged me to be better in games and have that extra confidence rather than take the easy option. To be exceptional and different, this is how you need to think. If it wasn't for Cyrille I would probably have just been an OK player trying to keep it simple. He helped me go to the next level.'

That 1991/92 season might have been even better had Villa managed to squeeze past an ailing Liverpool in the last eight of the FA Cup.

It took a masterful defence-splitting pass from John Barnes to cut Villa open midway into the second half, as advancing midfielder Michael Thomas finished clinically with a first-time strike. There had been very little in the tie at Anfield until that point, as Villa sniffed a route to Wembley under a manager who had tasted FA Cup success with Manchester United in 1983 and 1985.

The cup run, though, added to a much-improved league campaign and gave reason for great optimism among Villa supporters. They won their last three home games, including a vengeful 1-0 win over Liverpool courtesy of a Tony Daley goal. The Reds were minus the genius that was John Barnes but still had enough players with cup-winning pedigree. Villa, though, played rookies Matthias Breitkreutz, Ugo Ehiogu in just his eighth league game of a breakthrough season, the soon to be outgoing Ian Olney, and left-back Bryan Small in his sixth league match.

There was also a thumping 5-2 triumph in April against Tottenham at White Hart Lane after Villa had trailed 2-0 after 13 minutes. The signs were positive for the following season.

'We had some terrific results and we lost an FA Cup quarter-final 1-0 that we could and should have won,' Gray reflected. 'We were playing with a confidence in that campaign that led us to believe we could go there and upset them. I said to the guys in the dressing room before the game, "I've looked at the other teams in the last eight and if we beat Liverpool today, we will win this competition." I thoroughly believed that. That's how much better I thought we were than the rest. But for whatever reason we didn't play at our best.'

Ron Atkinson allowed Gray free rein to use his motivational skills in the dressing room and felt he was good at it. The players often responded.

'That was a typical Andy gee-up, to make us feel good and to have no fear,' skipper Kevin Richardson said with a smile. 'Even at Everton as a player he would be on to us in the dressing room and again on the field, either praising us for doing something well or giving us a rocket for not doing our jobs; he always wanted to win badly.

'So many teams went to Anfield in those days and were beaten before they went out, so he tried to instil some belief in the Villa team that day. It's hard to say if we were beaten before we went out; I don't know how the other lads were feeling but maybe one or two were lacking in confidence if they're being honest.

'I know it never quite felt like it did when I played for Everton, which is normal as derbies bring a different atmosphere. On those occasions I would probably think about the Liverpool players who I owed one or two tackles after they might have left their studs on me from the last encounter, so there would always be one or two thoughts of payback in my locker. It was like that in those days.'

Despite a prosperous season, Villa were struck a blow before the new campaign began when assistant manager Andy Gray told Atkinson he would be leaving the club to take up a full-time career in television. It was a decision he agonised over as he loved his work at Villa, where he had been a terrace hero since 1975.

'I had to go and talk to Ron about it, which I did,' Gray revealed. 'We sat down and had a chat. I told him that I was loving it, I loved working with the boys and couldn't get into training quick enough, I loved being there on matchdays standing next to Ron and learning from him. I saw it as my education. I was learning from one of the best and seeing what being a head coach is all about. I honestly thought that was going to be my path – until I got a call from a good friend who was putting together the Sky project.

'At the end of that first season we had, Sky won the rights to broadcast the Premier League and everyone who was working at BSB basically transferred over to Sky. They wanted me and made it clear that they could no longer allow me to combine my role at Villa with the television work, which I had been doing. It would be a full-time role, so I had a decision to make. I couldn't do that without sounding out the big man, Ron. He was as good as anything about it. He said, "Listen Andy, this is great now, but one minute you're flavour of the month and the next you're sacked. Television should be more secure for you and you won't have the same pressures on you as you would as a coach when you do this on your own. If I was you, I'd go." And I did. Ron and I were a good combination, I thought we worked well together, and he taught me a lot.

'Ron had even said to me, "Although you're not the main man here yet, if you keep learning, there's no doubt that one day my job could be yours." That was probably three of four years down the line. It was a very difficult summer making that decision and walking away from Aston Villa, which was a special club to me that was in my heart, and still is. Do I regret not staying and becoming the manager of Aston Villa further down the line? Sometimes, yes. Do I regret not staying on with Ron? Sometimes. We finished second the season after I left and maybe if I had stayed on, we might have won it. Maybe. Who knows? I don't know.'

If the relationship between manager and his assistant was always harmonious and full of mutual respect, the same cannot be said for Big Ron's relations with the chairman Doug Ellis.

Secretary Steve Stride had been at Villa since 1972 and had seen managers come and go over the years. He knew Ellis could be embarrassingly self-obsessed, egotistical, and sometimes boring. But he also knew how to deal with Ellis, and he tried to advise managers over the years that there was a right and wrong way to relate to the chairman. Most listened and took on the advice. Not Atkinson.

Stride said, 'I used to say to all managers, "If you want my advice, come down to the club on a Friday afternoon, tell Doug the team, talk about players and take him to a game occasionally." I didn't really need to say that to Graham Taylor because he was a shrewd man, but I did say that to all the others.

'I said Doug would love that. It was a hard balance for the managers though as Doug wasn't averse to tipping off the media about what the team was, so the managers stopped trusting him with the team.

'Also, I'd advise them that if they wanted a player, take Doug along to watch a game and if it was the left-back they wanted, casually say to Doug, "What do you think of the left-back, Doug?" And when Doug says he's good, say, "I hadn't really noticed Doug but you're right, he looks a proper player. Do you think we could get him?" Then Doug would go all out to sign the player the manager wanted all along but who Doug can tell everyone that he spotted! Ron wasn't so interested at playing these games with Doug and generally kept him at arm's length throughout his tenure.'

1991/92 season:

League position: 7th (of 22)

League Cup: second round (lost on away goals rule to Grimsby Town)

FA Cup: quarter-final (lost 1-0 at Liverpool)

Full Members' Cup: second round (lost 2-0 at home to Nottingham Forest)

Top scorers: Dwight Yorke 17; Cyrille Regis 11; Tony Daley 7

17

Bozzy, Ugo and Yorkie Offer Bright Future

'Vengloš was soft in his approach to the game and the boys took advantage of that, but with Big Ron, he made it clear that what he said goes and that was probably what we needed then.'

– Dwight Yorke

DEAN SAUNDERS, Andy Townsend, Steve Staunton, Ray Houghton, Kevin Richardson and more. Ron Atkinson brought many celebrated and successful footballers to Villa in his three years at the club, which was a refreshing change for supporters, who had become accustomed to signings who were likely to fulfil potential in the long run, as opposed to being the finished article straight away. If they were the finished product, they were probably on the back nine of their career like France international Didier Six in 1985, and in more recent years Peter Schmeichel, Robert Pires and John Terry.

Atkinson, though, had something of a Midas touch in attracting ready-made quality players to sign for his teams, especially during his time at Villa. But he also never took his eye off the future and appreciated that long-term development of talent was equally important.

At Manchester United, Atkinson signed Paul McGrath as a 22-year-old rookie from Ireland; he nurtured Norman Whiteside there and gave him a first-team debut two weeks before his 17th birthday to make him United's youngest player in 29 years, since Duncan Edwards. Big Ron always had an eye on the future, and he was no different at Villa.

He signed Australian Mark Bosnich at 20 years old and soon fast-tracked him to become his first-choice goalkeeper ahead of Nigel Spink. He played Dwight Yorke in 40 matches in his first season in 1991/92 in all competitions. Only six senior players appeared in more league games than Yorke, who finished as Villa's top scorer despite starting the campaign as a teenager. Left-back Bryan Small, who mostly deputised for Steve Staunton, also made his debut as a teenager in that season, while winger Steve Froggatt was handed a full league debut in a 0-0 draw at Arsenal while aged 18. The new signing from West Bromwich Albion, Ugo Ehiogu, made his first-team debut at 18, too, as Villa beat George Graham's very established and successful Arsenal side 3-1.

'There was a great crop of youth players coming through,' Tony Daley commented. 'Graham Taylor brought Yorkie over, but he started peaking under Ron. Dwight's one of the most talented players I ever played with, an incredible footballer.

'And what a goalkeeper Bosnich was. He might struggle in the modern game with a ball at his feet, but if you ask him to handle crosses and make saves, there were few better than him. He was unbelievable.

'Then Ugo, bless him. He defended like a trojan, was physically strong, had pace, was good in the air, another fantastic player, who probably had his best days under Brian Little at Villa.'

Yorke eventually signed for Manchester United in 1998 for £12.6m, having scored 98 goals for Villa in total. He was honest enough to say he left Villa Park purely to win trophies having won only a League Cup with the club in 1996. At United, he was a significant member of their treble-winning squad in 1999 when they won the Champions League, Premier League and FA Cup. He won the Premier League three times in three seasons.

But he owed his initial opportunity to Villa and the then manager Graham Taylor for spotting him on a mid-season tour of the Caribbean back in 1989, when the club subsequently signed him and gave him the chance to showcase his talents in England.

'We'd been told about this player before we went out there,' secretary Steve Stride remembered. 'Doug's version was that he sat on the bench next to Graham and asked him if he had noticed the number eight and Graham suddenly turned round and said, "No, but what a great player he is, chairman." Utter bollocks! They told us about him before we went out there. I can picture the scene now, Doug and I were sat in the only stand in the ground, behind the goal, no reserved VIP seats, which he obviously didn't like, and he was nowhere near Graham or the bench. But I know Graham did ask if Dwight could play for us after half-time, but his team said no chance. They felt if Dwight scored for Villa and they lost there would be a riot.'

The Yorke backstory is slightly deeper. He was soon to make his international debut for Trinidad and

Tobago as a 17-year-old after sparking much hype in the local media as the country's great new talent. Meantime, Villa embarked on a tour there because it was an international break. England were playing a World Cup qualifier in Albania on 8 March 1989, which they won 2-0 courtesy of goals from John Barnes and Bryan Robson. Villa therefore took advantage of the downtime in the English calendar.

Villa won the first game on 5 March 1-0 against Trinidad and Tobago in front of a crowd that was around one-third of the 30,000 capacity. It was normal for these tour fees to be paid at least 50 per cent in advance and Stride received payment by cash the day after in Trinidad after a member of the Trinidad and Tobago Football Association went with him to the bank and subsequently paid up.

Stride then set off to join the team in Tobago for their second match against a Tobago XI at Shaw Park, which Villa won 5-0 on 6 March. Stride flew on a four-seater charter plane with only one other passenger on board, none other than then FIFA Executive Committee member and soon to be CONCACAF president Jack Warner.

'At the time, we were one point away from qualifying for the 1990 World Cup and there was a lot of hype around the national team,' Yorke explained. 'I was still at school and didn't even do my GCSEs as I was focusing on football. This Villa match was a warm-up game we needed to play before our qualifier against America [which T&T subsequently lost 1-0 when they needed only a draw to qualify for Italia '90]. They provided us with the significant challenge that we needed.'

Yorke played in that match and the second friendly the next day in Tobago. 'It was a big deal for an English team to play out in Trinidad and Tobago and for me to be a starter in such a match with that kind of magnitude was quite incredible,' he added. 'Graham Taylor came into our dressing at half-time [in the Tobago match] and asked, "Can this kid play with us in the second half?" There was a big uproar about it and they told Graham that they couldn't take the best player from Tobago. The team manager was an airline ticket salesman, but he took it upon himself to take the role of my business manager and he insisted that if Villa were serious about me, they should give me a proper trial and take me to England.'

Villa agreed and subsequently signed Yorke on a two-year deal. He made just two appearances as a substitute under Graham Taylor, who then left for the England manager's job. There were then 21 appearances in all competitions under Jozef Vengloš, but his real breakthrough came under Ron Atkinson, who played him wide on the right, maybe three years before new manager Brian Little came in and started playing him as a striker.

'It was just very different playing for Ron,' Yorke added. 'As a player, you just want to play football but you realise you are playing for someone with a big personality and a big ego. I learned a lot from Ron being around, I have to say. Vengloš was soft in his approach to the game and the boys took advantage of that, but with Big Ron, he made it clear that what he said goes and that was probably what we needed then. He knew the English culture and had been an iconic manager at a club like Man United, so he had instant respect from the players. He was good for me and gave me a new contract. He saw that I had ability and all the tricks and felt I just needed more game time.'

Yorke might have been Villa's top scorer in 1991/92 but for a year or two after, his opportunities decreased once the strike partnership of Dean Saunders and Dalian Atkinson began to thrive. There was also Ray Houghton and Tony Daley competing with Yorke for the wide-right position. However, Yorke felt that while it was frustrating at the time to sit out rather than play, he learned so much.

'That was a key time in my development because I had to learn about the game on the training ground or while I was sitting on the bench,' Yorke said. 'Learning from Deano and his movements in the box and how he scores his goals; how Dalian manoeuvres himself to go past people with his power and pace, though his end product was not always sublime. I was slowly navigating myself through this and taking the good bits from all these players and adding them to what I could become myself. Nowadays I might have gone out on loan, but I was never allowed to go on loan at Villa, which I guess is a compliment as it meant the manager wanted me around. There were loads of clubs that wanted me on loan.'

Bosnich, who soon became Yorke's best friend at Villa as they enjoyed the Birmingham social life together, made his Manchester United first-team debut at 18 in a goalless draw in April 1990 against Wimbledon. He was highly regarded at Old Trafford as Alex Ferguson sought a replacement for Jim Leighton. But visa rules – Bosnich hadn't played enough first-team football for United – blocked a long-term move.

Enter Big Ron and his large network of contacts from within the game.

Atkinson said, 'A guy called Graham Smith, who was a goalkeeper that played for me at Cambridge as well as for the likes of West Brom and Colchester, rang me and said, "What do you think of the lad Bosnich?" I knew he'd been at Man United but didn't know much about him. Fortunately, I had Brian Whitehouse on my staff who knew the reserves scene well and I asked him about Bosnich, and he said, "I know him well, if you can get him, do not hesitate!"

'I had Andy Gray speak to his Scotland international team-mate Jim Leighton about him and Jim said he's the best young goalie he's ever seen, so we started looking into the ins and outs of why he left United. It turns out he had been on a scholarship scheme and Alex wanted him to go and play in Europe to earn his visa points to qualify for a proper contract. But he went home instead.

'We had a solicitor advising us out of Hong Kong and amidst all our conversations on what can we do to sign Bosnich, I thought of something I had seen in Spain and said, "Has the lad got a girlfriend?" They said he had a girlfriend in Manchester, and I asked,

"Would he marry her?" So, after several conversations between England and Australia, he married her, and the rest is history.' Steve Stride then flew out to Australia to complete the paperwork.

'When he came over it was clear he had been living like a beach bum and enjoying the Sydney lifestyle a bit too much,' continued Big Ron. 'He wasn't fit and I thought to myself, "Bloody hell, what have we signed here?" But gradually he shaped up and eventually he proved himself to be one of my best signings. His big chance [having already played 17 matches in the first team in 1992/93] arrived in the League Cup against Birmingham City when Spinky got sent off and Bozzy came on and saved a John Frain penalty.

'As Bozzy was given more opportunities it became clear we had signed a top keeper. He had to bide his time though as Spinky was still a top keeper and I didn't drop him straight away. Besides, Spinky also had the advantage of being English so was an automatic pick for the European games.

'People questioned his kicking, but it never bothered me. I remember we went on a pre-season tour to Japan. We were playing an eight-a-side game with big goals. Dean Saunders was doing everything he could to score, headers, volleys, shots, and in the end, Dean turned round to me and said, "How the effing hell do you beat this fella?" That was Bozzy who I rate as Villa's best-ever goalkeeper, and I've seen all of them since the '50s.'

Bosnich left Villa in 1999 after seven great seasons there, returning to Manchester United where it all started for him. Sadly for Bosnich, he was not able to replicate his Villa form and was transferred 18 months later to Chelsea, where he also never did his talents justice.

The signing of Ugo Ehiogu was equally shrewd from Villa, or especially Atkinson. He knew Paul McGrath and Shaun Teale were his first-choice centre-halves and he had the potential for Earl Barrett to move into the middle, if necessary. But he wanted to add cover for all those positions. Ehiogu was something of an opportunist raid.

'We had a good youth team at Sheffield Wednesday and even beat the Class of '92,' Atkinson recalled. 'We played the Albion on a cup run and we were beating them 3-0 but it would have been six if it wasn't for this big centre-half they had. All of a sudden, they moved him into midfield, and he scored. Then they put him at centre-forward with about five minutes left and he scored again. I was thinking, "If this game goes on any longer, we'll get beat here." Anyway, the game finished 3-2.

'I got hold of Talby [West Brom manager Brian Talbot] after the match and said, "Hey, any chance of us taking that lad Ehiogu?" He said, "No chance." Anyway, at the end of the season Talby got the sack and he rang me and said Ehiogu's contract was up and he didn't wish to play for the club any more. I told him to get the player to write to me, Brian Clough and someone else I can't remember and ask for a trial. I knew that would be useful if it went to a tribunal. I knew [David] Wetherall and [Jon] Newsome had been tapped up by Howard Wilkinson to go to Leeds and I thought Ugo will fill that role nicely. Then about the same time I got the Villa job and had to call Talby to say, "Tell the lad to re-address his letter to me at Villa Park." They had the tribunal at Villa Park and Bobby Gould and Stuart "Pancho" Pearson were there to represent the Albion. Pancho was my mate. I took him to the Albion specifically to work with Don Goodman! Pancho said, "Ron, are you coming into the tribunal?" I said, "You what, he's a fuckin' youth team player. Of course I'm not."

'I played it down a treat because I knew if I went in it would make the player look more important, so I sent our youth coach in to say, "The player has written to us, and we're prepared to give him his chance." The youth coach told me afterwards, "Forty grand." I tried to act disappointed, but I wasn't kidding anyone. Pancho dropped in and said, with a knowing smile, "You bastard! You've done us like a kipper." They had gone in trying to argue Ugo was another Duncan Edwards. In pre-season it quickly became obvious we'd got a good one, from the way he was launching into those tackles of his.'

Ehiogu, languid and cool on the ball and a magnificent tackler with his long legs, ended up with four England caps and was the reason Middlesbrough broke their transfer record when spending £8m on him in 2000. First, though, he had a great career at Villa, where he clocked up 303 appearances in all competitions.

He wasn't always good at Villa straight away, though, as Atkinson recalled one of his early matches at home against Norwich City, who won 3-2 in November 1992.

'He had an absolute mare and I had to take him off late on,' Big Ron said. 'In the dressing room afterwards, I said, "We've got a presentation to make here, lads. Ugo has just been named as Norwich's player of the month!" He could take a joke, fortunately.'

18

Deano and the Baker's Dozen

'I was raging in that [Liverpool] game. I always played for the manager and once Graeme Souness showed a sign that he was prepared to let me go, I was out to prove a point.'

– Dean Saunders

VILLA WERE 15th after the first six league matches of the 1992/93 season. They won just two of their opening eight games, drawing four and losing two. It was not exactly the kind of start that demonstrated here was a team that would be challenging for the title. But then something happened, which changed the whole expectation level at the club and radically improved results. Dean Saunders signed.

'I knew once Ron brought Dean Saunders in, they would be challenging for the title,' the former assistant manager Andy Gray said. 'That was a huge signing for Villa.'

The impact of Saunders' £2.3m arrival was immediate. He scored two goals on his home debut – against the team that had sold him, Liverpool – then added four more in his next two league matches: two at Middlesbrough and two at Wimbledon. Atkinson had been scouring the whole of Europe to find his goal machine and now, he had found him at last in the shape of the Wales international, who he had been an admirer of for some time.

'I was tipped off in 1988 by a mate of mine [who was a director at Oxford United] about Dean when they were selling him to Derby,' Atkinson recalled. 'He told me he had doubts about some players they had sold on, but he had no doubts whatsoever about Saunders. I said to him, "Now you're telling me!" I had left United by then anyway, but it's always interesting to hear about any gems going around. Then I watched him do well at Derby and eventually Liverpool, so Deano had been on my radar for quite some time. I was thankful to finally work with him at Villa. I was lucky in the same way as with Stan [Steve Staunton] that Souey [Liverpool boss Graeme Souness] was looking to sell a few of his non-English players. He had to make spaces in his squad for English players.'

The Saunders transfer almost never happened after a long, drawn-out process had started to irritate the decision-makers at Anfield.

'We agreed a deal between myself and Souey and this thing went on for about two weeks,' Big Ron revealed. 'I was always of the opinion that if a deal is going to get done it usually happens fairly quickly. The last straw for me was when Souey told me, "Ron, I'm thinking of selling Rushy [Ian Rush] and keeping Deano." He might have been playing games to move things on, but I don't think he was.

'I had to tell Doug to get it done. I think he was quibbling over ten grand in the end. Deano was calling me as well asking what was going on. I'd had him down at my house telling him stories and he loved it, and he was ready to move so he didn't want it collapsing either. The fans were having a go at Doug on a local radio phone-in on the Friday night as we'd lost at home to Chelsea in midweek. On the Saturday morning, I was driving to our game to play Crystal Palace and Steve Stride called me up saying, "The chairman wants to know what the deal is with Saunders." I said, "The same as it was two weeks ago, but I think Souey is getting fed up and might pull out." Shortly after, Steve called me back to say that Doug was going to speak to Peter Robinson [Liverpool's chief executive at the time] there and then. By the time I reached the ground the deal was done. Once that was confirmed I asked for a mic and walked on to the pitch and announced the Saunders signing. Maybe I was a bit premature, but I wanted the crowd to get behind us when they were threatening to turn. We won that day 3-0 even though we never played that well, but the feelgood factor got us over the line.'

The irony of how football fixtures crop up at particular times is quite incredible. Atkinson's first match as Villa boss against Sheffield Wednesday, the club he had just left amid great acrimony, was one such example; Garry Thompson's debut goal for Crystal Palace against his former team and boyhood club Villa to help thwart their title bid in 1989/90 was another. Dean Saunders' home debut at Villa Park just had to be against Liverpool, of course. Villa would probably have been the one club Souness would rather not have played then given they had Saunders, Ray Houghton and Steve Staunton in their line-up, all disaffected Reds rejects, to put it crudely, all desperate to show the Scot he was wrong to sell them. The match finished

4-2 to Villa, despite the visitors taking the lead in the 43rd minute courtesy of ex-Villa player Mark Walters. By the time Ronny Rosenthal scored an 84th-minute consolation goal, the contest was already over. Israel international Rosenthal is more renowned in that game for his so-called 'miss of the season' – having struck the crossbar after beating Shaun Teale to the ball and then rounding goalkeeper Nigel Spink only to blast the ball at the woodwork in front of the Holte End. The game, though, belonged to Saunders.

'I was raging,' the Welshman said. 'I always played for the manager and once the Liverpool manager Graeme Souness showed a sign that he was prepared to let me go, I was out to prove a point.

'I said to Graeme, once he made it clear he was happy to see me leave, "So you're really going to let me speak to Ron Atkinson?" He said, "Yeah." I told him, "You're making a massive mistake. I'm in your corner."

'The feeling I was getting from both managers couldn't have been more different. Ron was telling me he was going to make me great and how I was going to help push Villa on to the next level with my goals. With all the great players he had already assembled – he said I was the missing link. He said, "You know Ray [Houghton], Steve [Staunton], we've got Garry

Parker, Paul McGrath, two good goalkeepers, Dalian is something else. You're going to love it here." I was sold on Villa then.

'Ron never told us to take a step back and let the opposition have the ball. We were always on the front foot having a go. He would always say to us at half-time if we were having one of our languid performances, "Who's driving the bus? We've got too many passengers. Get on the front foot, make the difference. I want ten bus drivers out there!"'

The Liverpool result was the third match in a 13-game unbeaten run for Villa, which elevated them to third in the table before a deflating 3-2 loss at home to Norwich City, the infamous match in which Atkinson humorously denigrated the below-par display of young defender Ugo Ehiogu. The Canaries did the double over Villa that season and were one of the reasons why their titles hopes were ultimately dented.

Captain Kevin Richardson was the manager's most vocal policeman on the field and he was frustrated by the team's occasional lapses like at home to Norwich, when, for whatever reason, they just switched off when they had been playing amazing football as a unit.

'We were producing big results against big clubs,' Richardson said, 'and I would say, "Why can't we do this more often, lads? That belief and level of performance has to be there every week against the big clubs and the not-so-big teams," which was something that let us down occasionally like against Norwich. Gradually, I felt individually the players were realising what we had as a group. We were a team of talented individuals that was coming together well. I had won the league before at Everton and Arsenal and I believed we had what it took.'

Two weeks after the Liverpool victory, there was more reason for supporters to eulogise over Villa's achievements, but this time from Saunders' strike partner Dalian Atkinson. He scored the third goal in a 3-2 win that was later voted as *Match of the Day*'s goal of the season. In a match played in driving rain, he received the ball, rolled Lawrie Sanchez, skipped past the sliding challenge of Scott Fitzgerald, came inside Gary Elkins, recovered after a bad touch almost allowed Elkins a second opportunity to tackle him but instead he went outside of his challenge, and, as space opened up, John Scales approached Atkinson before a shimmy persuaded him to jockey rather than tackle and Atkinson then just dinked a deft chip over goalkeeper Hans Segers from 20 yards.

A celebration followed that became infamous in Villa folklore. Supporter Martin Pritchard, now known among fans as 'Rain Man', dashed on to the pitch to hold an umbrella over Atkinson and Saunders, who had piggy-backed his fellow striker in the celebrations. It later became known that Pritchard was allowed to sit at the front of the away end because he had an ankle injury.

'You cannot forget that,' Richardson recalled. 'Other players were shouting at him for the ball, but Dalian just had it in his head that he was going alone. He had the ability to do that and tried it on other occasions and lost the ball and he would have been hammered by everyone. Even that day, when he scored at Wimbledon, I remember thinking, "Dalian's doing his thing again, when is he going to lose it, I'd better be in position ready to defend." What he did, though, to just dink the goalie rather than try a proper shot, where do you get that kind of confidence from? It was incredible. When the fan came over with that umbrella, if he had given Dalian a microphone, he would probably have sung a song. He had amazing confidence.'

On the partnership that was forming menacingly between Saunders and Dalian Atkinson, Richardson added, 'Dean was a very intelligent striker. His knowledge of knowing when to go behind, when to drop deep, when to go wide, he got some great goals for Villa. His character was also very good. The combination he had with Dalian worked a treat. They always seemed to know where each other were. It was a really good partnership. The fans must have thought, "Wow, we've not seen an attacking combination like this since Peter Withe and Gary Shaw" when Villa won the European Cup.'

19

Souey's Regrets

'I made loads of mistakes. Letting Steve Staunton move to Aston Villa for £1.1m just after I arrived was definitely one of them.'

– Graeme Souness

THE SIGNING of Dean Saunders, six weeks after Ray Houghton had made the same switch down the M6 from the north-west to Birmingham, crystallised something to Villa supporters: the generosity of Reds manager Graeme Souness, who had also sold left-back Steve Staunton to Villa more than a year earlier.

Villa fans had been accustomed over the years to not expecting big names or established stars brought in, mostly because chairman Doug Ellis was unwilling to pay large wages or even bloated transfer fees. Even when Villa won the European Cup (when Ellis was not in power), there were no stars in the team. The match-winner Peter Withe had been signed from Newcastle United with a reputation as a handy journeyman more than anything else.

However, the arrival of Ron Atkinson changed the landscape. He was not at Villa to finish in mid-table. He wanted, in his own words, 'to have a right go at the title' which had eluded him when he was Manchester United boss.

The trio of Wales striker Saunders, creative Republic of Ireland midfielder Houghton and his countryman Staunton were a major factor in Villa's upward curve in the 1992/93 campaign which took them agonisingly close to winning the league.

Curiously, Liverpool at that time were starting a 30-year cycle without winning the First Division, or the Premier League as it became in 1992. They were runners-up on five occasions in that period but, as Villa are aware, nobody remembers second.

The initial capture of Staunton was something of a fluke for Big Ron as he wasn't his first choice.

'I made an enquiry for David Burrows with Graeme Souness as I knew him from West Brom,' Ron explained. 'This was a time when you had to try to maintain a majority of British players for European competition. You were allowed only three non-English players in your team unless they were developed here. Graeme at that time had three left-backs, Gary Ablett, Burrows and Stan [Staunton], who was the odd one out on the European rule. Staunton became a conversation piece as often happened between managers. Sometimes, you start discussing one player and different players come into the conversation.'

Souness acknowledged the European rule was the main reason he allowed the Irish left-back to join Villa. The deal was tied up when Atkinson and Staunton met at a hotel off junction seven of the M6.

'I made loads of mistakes,' Souness admitted. 'Letting Steve Staunton move to Aston Villa for £1.1m just after I arrived was definitely one of them. With hindsight, my thinking was too heavily influenced by the stupid rule in force at the time that classed Irish, Scottish and Welsh players as foreigners. You weren't allowed more than three in your team for European games. I also had David Burrows, who looked like he could become England's left-back at the time, and I thought he could only get better because he was in his early 20s. Steve was a very good player and turned out to be a great one, so letting him go was a big mistake, but it was partly forced on me.'

The Glasgow-born Republic of Ireland midfielder Ray Houghton was next through the Villa door from Liverpool, this time for £900,000. Souness never had the reason for selling him that he had for Staunton because he was English-qualified in Europe as he had been an apprentice at West Ham United in his early days.

One thing Houghton brought to Villa was a winning pedigree. While in 1990, when Villa fell short of the title possibly due to a lack of experience at handling that pressure at the top of the league, the 1992/93 season was looking different with more medal winners in the ranks. Houghton won a medal every year he was at Anfield, including two league titles, two FA Cups and a Charity Shield (known as the Community Shield since 2002). Even the year before he joined Liverpool, the man known as 'Razor' won the League Cup with Oxford United in 1986.

For just £900,000, Houghton, then aged 30 and in his prime as an industrious midfielder, seemed a very shrewd buy for Villa, especially after he had just won an FA Cup and finished as Liverpool's second-highest goalscorer behind Saunders. It seemed the emergence of Steve McManaman softened the blow for Reds fans, while Souness never wanted to hold on to any player who felt they would be better off at any other club.

'Souey was going through a bit of a transition, and we probably benefitted from that,' Atkinson commented. 'I always said the best player in that right midfield position was Gordon Strachan, he was a genius, and Ray was the closest thing to Strach. Ray was a very intelligent player. I picked the phone up to Souey and said, "How much is Ray going to cost us?" Once I had a starting figure, I'd hand it over to Doug to finish it off. Doug would always try to get a deal a bit cheaper than what I had told him it would be, but he was unlikely to chip [chief executive] Peter Robinson down in price, as he was a hard negotiator himself.'

Souness maintained that his motivation for letting Houghton leave was more about the player not wanting to be at Anfield any longer, which was a feeling he didn't have any time for.

'Ray Houghton told me his wife was homesick and wanted to go back to London,' Souness recalled. 'We agreed a deal with Chelsea, and he was going to see them that day, when I got a call from him saying, "Ron Atkinson wants to talk to me. Can I speak to him?"

'"I thought you were homesick," I said. There was silence on the other end of the phone. At that time my attitude to it all was, "If you want to leave, go." I still thought of Liverpool as the best place to be in European football. That was how I remembered the club. Obviously, these lads felt differently. I was too impetuous, though. I should have said, "I hear you. Let me get players in to replace you," because there was still a bit of life in them … Steve McMahon, Peter Beardsley and Ray Houghton were allowed to leave, not because they were no longer any good, but because they had told me they had wanted to go, but I should have been stronger and resisted until I had replacements for them.'

Dean Saunders was the sale that hurt Souness most in hindsight. He now admits he was wrong to offload him to Villa, but at the time he was fighting an internal battle where senior players were hanging on to their status as leading players in the club and he was conflicted in trying to placate them on one hand but secretly wanted to change things up on the other.

In fact, within a week of Souness signing Saunders from Derby County he had his former team-mate and goalscoring legend Ian Rush at his door because he had found out that Saunders was being paid slightly more money than him.

'Dean was one of my regrets at Liverpool,' Souness admitted. 'He scored 23 goals in one year there, but I had other players, big-name players at the club, telling me they couldn't play with him, so I stupidly let him go and he went to Villa. I got Dean back when I went to Galatasaray and wherever I've had him after that, either as a player or coach, he's been outstanding for me on and off the pitch.'

Saunders was shocked on hearing that Liverpool were prepared to sell him to Villa, especially as he had scored in his last game for the Reds, against Chelsea.

'I was surprised, as I'd scored 23 goals the season before and beat Roger Hunt's record for most goals by a Liverpool player in a European campaign. I got nine, which was a club record until [Roberto] Firmino and [Mo] Salah went past me,' Saunders said.

'But once I knew Liverpool didn't want me, I was happy to sign for Villa. Big Ron just knows what to say to players. I was aware he'd gone on the pitch and announced he was trying to sign me. Classic Ron.

'I took quite a hefty wage cut to sign for Villa actually, but Ron said to me, "I can't pay you any more than that but if you do well, I will put your wages back to the way they were at Liverpool." I said, "OK."'

There remained a healthy respect between Saunders and Souness, however, and in fact the Welshman earned even more of the Scot's respect after he heard the striker's reaction when approached by a journalist who was sniffing an opportunity for an interview with a disaffected player bombed out of Liverpool.

'Graeme signed me five times: Liverpool, Galatasaray, Benfica, Blackburn as assistant manager and Newcastle as assistant manager. That proved there was no bad blood between us after he sold me to Villa, as he took me to five different clubs,' Saunders enthused.

'He re-signed me for Galatasaray as he had put a buyback release clause in my contract when he sold me to Villa that if any foreign club bid £2.5m they could buy me with a staggered transfer payment.

'I know he regretted selling me to Villa as his wife, Karen, told me. We were in a restaurant in Turkey. She told me that he got to find out that a journalist from *The Sun* offered me a lot of money when I left Liverpool to slag Graeme off and I refused. The reporter apparently told Graeme that and when he got to hear he felt even worse about selling me. And I started scoring at Villa straight away.

'But I have nothing but good things to say about Graeme Souness. A great bloke, a great manager, and he just made a judgement call at the time. He was trying to raise some money as we were forced to play all the youngsters when we had a load of injuries and my sale helped him to do that. But in hindsight he tried to change things too soon.'

Saunders scored two goals on his Villa debut against Liverpool. There was a quick realisation among the players that Atkinson had brought in a serious finisher, maybe even the missing link; or as Ron Saunders phrased it on signing Peter Withe in 1980, the last piece in the jigsaw. They were now ready to have a genuine crack at the title.

'Sometimes that happens,' skipper Kevin Richardson said. 'Managers get rid of players and then they think, "Oh shit, I should have kept him." Dean was desperate to do well for Villa and show Souness that he was wrong to let him go. His work rate and his goals were incredible. His Villa debut must have been a very satisfying day for him.'

20

Fergie Time Sparks Villa Implosion

'I said, "I'll tell you now, they will play until they win." Sure enough, they won 2-1, Brucey got them both. That was the start of "Fergie Time". They were a better team than us, fair enough. But the pressure was all on them at that time and that was the first moment when I thought, "I think this title race might just be slipping away."'

– Ron Atkinson

IF ANYONE really wanted to know how much Ron Atkinson believed his Villa team were worthy title contenders prior to the 1992/93 season, which was the inaugural Premier League campaign, they only need to read the following admittance from the manager.

'I had a lot of money on it,' Big Ron revealed. 'We couldn't do it now with all these betting rules and regulations that are in place, but at the time me and Macca had a bet that we would win the league. The odds were ridiculous, something like 50/1, and I knew we would be in the frame at the very least. I think, if my memory serves me right, we put a grand down. We laid it all off in the end and still got more than our money back!'

Bets by football players and managers nowadays are strictly forbidden, though at least back then Atkinson was piling money on his own team to win. It would have been controversial if he'd backed any *other* club.

In the event, as we now know, Villa lost their last three matches to Blackburn Rovers, Oldham Athletic and Queens Park Rangers and couldn't take the fight to the end. Manchester United, meanwhile, did not lose any of their last ten league games, winning the final seven. It was the start of more than a decade of domination at the top of English football by Alex Ferguson's Red Devils.

Ferguson had assembled a formidable squad of experienced players such as Steve Bruce, Bryan Robson, Mark Hughes, Gary Pallister, Paul Ince,

Peter Schmeichel, Paul Parker, Denis Irwin, Brian McClair, Eric Cantona, and youth in the shape of Ryan Giggs and Lee Sharpe. The so-called Class of '92 lay in wait and were ready to filter through into the first team when they came of age in the manager's eyes: Paul Scholes, David Beckham, Gary and Phil Neville, and Nicky Butt added to the quality over the next few seasons as the experienced players were ruthlessly phased out by Fergie.

But as good as United were, Villa matched them for most of that season. Big Ron's men were top of the league in early April. Ultimately, though, too many poor results cost them dearly and against clubs they would have been expected to beat. It was a feature of their season, sporadically. Even Norwich City led the table at the business end due to Villa's inconsistencies. Yet it had been a tale of great expectation for much of that campaign.

Once Dean Saunders joined in September, leading to their 13-match unbeaten streak, there was a real momentum about Villa. A 2-1 win at Anfield on 9 January to give them the league double over Liverpool seemed a watershed moment, just like it had been in 1981, when Villa last won the league. On that occasion, Villa had beaten Liverpool 2-0 at home, and it was the result that gave players genuine belief. This was no different once goals from Garry Parker and Saunders had cancelled out John Barnes's earlier strike. Villa went second with the win and moved into first place a week later for the first time that season after thrashing Middlesbrough 5-1 at home.

The legendary manager in 1981, Ron Saunders, always identified Liverpool as the benchmark of greatness. He felt if his side measured up to them, they were doing all right. Strangely, only due to their achievements over the previous 15 years did the Reds retain that reputation. There was a power shift taking place in English football, and Villa were fighting to stake their claim at the top table, along with Manchester United, Arsenal and Liverpool. Norwich were the outliers, even more so than Villa in this season.

Big Ron claimed Anfield was his lucky ground. He even won there twice as manager of Coventry City, with Peter Ndlovu scoring a hat-trick in 1995 in a 3-2 win against the likes of David James, Jan Mølby, Steve McManaman, Ian Rush and Robbie Fowler. Ron also took all the points at Liverpool in his first season as Manchester United manager in 1981 courtesy of goals from Kevin Moran and Arthur Albiston, while

Frank Stapleton scored the only goal there in 1985. Karma evened things up somewhat in 1989, when his Sheffield Wednesday side were hammered 5-1 shortly after he had taken over at Hillsborough.

'When you went to Anfield, you had to be on it for 90 minutes with a full tank of petrol,' Villa skipper Kevin Richardson commented. 'Work your bollocks off, no dropping off. We did that. It felt like the tide was turning and they were starting to worry about the threat that we had.

'I remember playing against Michael Thomas in midfield that day as we were mates from our Arsenal days. He used to float around, and I'd say to him, "Hey Mickey, you just having a rest today, you not going to do any running?" There were a lot of changes going on at Liverpool and maybe they hadn't come to grips with them by this time, I don't know. But we were playing well.'

It's true that Paul Stewart, Michael Thomas, Jamie Redknapp and an ageing Barnes was a far cry from the midfield of years past like Steve McMahon, Ronnie Whelan, Jan Mølby and Ray Houghton. But any win at Anfield was regarded as one to savour.

If obscure and peculiar results eventually cost Villa, there had to be a reason. Didn't there?

Random poor results do not just happen from nowhere. Maybe as a one-off but not repeatedly. The consensus among that squad was that injury to key striker Dalian Atkinson was one of the two main blows that killed off their title chances. The speedy centre-forward was known to be mercurial and magical as much as lazy and inconsistent, yet all the players and the manager loved him. He did the unbelievable, like his special goal at Wimbledon, and all top teams possessed that kind of influence. United had Cantona, Liverpool once had Kenny Dalglish and Villa, in '81, had Tony Morley. Dalian Atkinson was now 'it'.

However, between 5 December – when he scored both goals in a 2-1 win against his former club Sheffield Wednesday – and 4 April, Dalian featured in only three matches (a draw at Manchester City and away wins at Liverpool and Chelsea) with several weeks separating all of those appearances. He was substituted in all three and Villa's momentum was suffering because of his extended absence.

'His injury in that season was a significant factor why we never won the league,' Dean Saunders reflected. 'If he was at the races, he could be unplayable.'

Richardson concurred, 'He was a big loss, who could replace Dalian? He was our best player and to lose him then when you need to keep churning out the results, that was a huge blow. The other lads tried, and it was nobody's fault, but they couldn't replicate the kind of threat that Dalian had. You could see the visible fear on defenders' faces when Dalian got the ball. It was like, "Bloody hell, not him, what's he going to do next?" Even Dalian didn't know what he was going to do. His trickery, his pace, his power, his one-twos with Deano. There was a big hole left when he wasn't in the team.'

'Deano and Dalian' hit it off straight away and it was no fluke as the manager had plotted it all; first tactically with both signings and then psychologically, by coercing the friendship. It was Big Ron's decision to room them together when on away trips.

'Ron wanted me to get into Dalian's head because he was adamant that if my work rate could rub off on him, he would be a world beater,' Saunders quipped.

'I told Dalian, "I'll do all the running and you take all the whacks" – because he was so strong that defenders used to bounce off him. Quite often I'd run off him and pick up the loose balls that he won off the defenders. Dalian put his hands together as if he was praying and said, "Oh my God, I've been waiting to hear that all my career." He was so funny. He used to shout to me during games, "Deano! Deano! I'm fucked! I can't fucking breathe!" He had asthma, in fact we both had asthma. I used to take my inhaler on the pitch with me and I would throw it to him when he was struggling.

'He was so funny. He had a Lotus Carlton and it was pretty much a racing car. He would often get pulled over by the police. This one time, he was pulled over and they said to him, "Sir, we clocked you speeding at 100mph." He said, "No, you've got it wrong. I got it up to 140 at one point!" Can you believe that! He got insulted because the police thought he was only doing 100mph. He was so funny, bless him. We all loved him.'

One particularly damaging and costly result for Villa that Dalian missed came at Highfield Road on Boxing Day when Midlands rivals Coventry City won 3-0 after Micky Quinn (two) and Robert Rosario scored three goals in seven chaotic minutes. Sky Blues manager Bobby Gould was at it again, masterminding another win over Villa after he had done the same on several occasions when he was Wimbledon boss.

It's ironic in some ways how Villa's league title bid faltered in both the 1989/90 and 1992/93 seasons with similarly poor results. In each campaign they lost 1-0 at Crystal Palace at a key time; they slipped to 2-0 and 3-0 losses at Coventry; there were home and away defeats to Norwich in 1992/93, and a loss and draw to the Canaries in 1989/90; uncharacteristically disappointing defeats to QPR in both seasons; and, to crystallise the comparison, there were shock losses to Oldham, in the FA Cup in 1990 and league title run-in three years later. An uncanny set of results that typified Villa's lack of consistency and ruthlessness to get the job done under pressure when so close to creating history.

'It was a mystery,' Richardson admitted. 'After the results we had been getting against top clubs, those games were unacceptable. Where did those performances come from? Was it swagger? Over-confidence? We'll probably never know. The best players aren't good one week and shit the next. You can tell yourselves how good you are when that cup is in your hand.

'It was very frustrating. Especially as I had won the league before with both Everton and Arsenal and I think there was more flair, skill and ability among that

Villa team than what Arsenal had. They had David Rocastle and Paul Merson, while Paul Davis made good late runs for goals, but Arsenal's success was more down to a disciplined team structure with everyone doing their jobs well. George Graham worked so hard on our defence. It wasn't hard to see why we were successful defensively. We caught people offside loads of times. That defence, led by Tony Adams, was very reliable. But like I say I don't think that Arsenal side had the same enterprise that the Villa had.'

Tony Daley also felt that Villa 'had a better team all-round under Big Ron' than the team he had played in under Graham Taylor that finished second in 1990. He enjoyed 1989/90 more purely because he had greater involvement and relished the fact they were punching above their weight and surprising everyone. This time, in 1992/93, there was expectation.

On 10 April 1993 and a month out from the end of the season, Coventry dealt Villa another painful blow when they held them to a goalless draw at Villa Park to knock Big Ron's team off top spot for the final time in that campaign. They would never return to the summit.

It summed up Villa's inability to finish off their fine season for Coventry had lost at Villa Park in all three previous meetings there and had never won in the league at Villa in their history dating back to 1936. Coventry were supposed to be Villa's lucky team. But no, the Sky Blues had the resolve to steal a point.

'We should have beaten them,' a still angry Dwight Yorke reflected. 'It was a missed opportunity. We felt we could push United all the way.

'When you think of those key games we lost towards the end of the season, we really let ourselves down. Norwich away was always going to be a test but we should still have won that game. Drawing at home to Coventry wasn't good enough, then those three defeats at the end starting at Blackburn, not good enough but it seems like it was done by then. When you think about what we were playing for, the Premier League title, we should have been better. Three points had to be the only outcome.

'Blackburn away, Norwich away, they were always going to be tricky, but there can be no excuses for not beating Coventry at home, which upset our momentum.'

That day, when Villa played Coventry at home, was famous for another moment in time from the campaign: 'Fergie Time' was born.

The now famous image of a frantic, even angry Alex Ferguson on the touchline, checking his wristwatch, possibly to show the officials he is expecting more time for United to score a goal when they most need one, is legendary. But it was on that day when it really entered folklore.

Ron Atkinson remembered, 'We had played Coventry, drew, and someone in the crowd said, "Ron, United are getting beat by Sheffield Wednesday." By the time we reached the dressing room someone else told me they'd equalised. I said, "I'll tell you now, they will play until they win." Sure enough, they won 2-1, Brucey [Steve Bruce] got them both. That was the start of "Fergie Time". They were a better team than us, fair enough. But the pressure was all on them at that time and that was the first moment when I thought, "I think this title race might just be slipping away." There's always a moment when these things turn and that was it. If they had got beat the bottom would have fell out of them. Carlton Palmer is a good friend of mine, he was playing in that game. Carlton told me that he went up to the referee and asked how long was left. He was told two minutes of stoppage time. Six minutes later, Wednesday were still winning, but not for long!'

'Those two goals from Brucey really cost us,' Dean Saunders said. 'I thought we were going to win the league. If Dalian hadn't got injured, and without Fergie Time, I think we'd have done it.'

Villa bounced back from the Coventry match by going to Highbury and winning 1-0 courtesy of a Tony Daley goal against George Graham's Arsenal, as they did in 1990 when Chris Price scored in the title run-in. They followed that up with a 3-1 home victory over Manchester City.

At this stage, Manchester United were on 75 points after 39 games and Villa were just a point behind on 74, with both teams having three matches remaining. United were in the ascendancy with that one-point advantage and a far superior goal difference. But it was up to Villa to keep the pressure on and take the race to the last game. The inaugural Premier League had the potential to be a spectacle of a climax. But it turned out to be a predictable ending as Villa folded meekly.

United, who hadn't managed to beat Villa after three attempts that season with away losses in the League Cup and the league and a draw at Old Trafford, won 2-0 at Palace, beat Blackburn 3-1 at home, and then edged Wimbledon 2-1 when the title was already wrapped up.

Villa slipped to a 3-0 defeat at Ewood Park, a 1-0 defeat at home to Oldham, and then a season-ending

2-1 loss at Loftus Road. 'That Blackburn result is the moment that sticks with me more than anything from that season, unfortunately,' Ray Houghton said. 'I remember being on the field and feeling helpless as they kept scoring and I was thinking, "What the hell is going on?" It was just terrible and was a sorry way for our season to end, effectively.'

Mike Newell and Kevin Gallacher put Blackburn 2-0 up in the first quarter of an hour and Newell added his second five minutes before half-time. That was game over, season over, even before Big Ron could begin his team talk.

'For the first 20 minutes we played them off the park, absolutely battered them,' Atkinson said. 'Dalian missed two or three good chances, yet they still managed to go 2-0 up quite early on from sucker punches and I was sitting there thinking, "What the hell is going on here?"'

Saunders added, 'Our chance was gone after the Blackburn game pretty much. That game killed us, we lost momentum and we started to doubt ourselves.'

'It was like a whirlwind in the first half,' Kevin Richardson added. 'Whether players did anything different in the build-up to that game, I'm not sure, but we were really off the pace. I would be curious now that if we all got together in a room and asked "What happened?", what kind of answers would come back.'

Dwight Yorke maintains Villa 'were definitely good enough' to have won the league that season, but a mixture of poor self-belief and selections cost them.

'Ron mainly stayed true to his tried and trusted players,' Yorke said. 'I felt there were games where he could have played me, sometimes ahead of Dalian, and he didn't. One game I seem to remember where there was a big argument in the dressing room was the Blackburn away match. Ron played Bryan Small and Steve Staunton, who was out wide on the left. Some of the senior players felt I should have played. I listened to it all but kept quiet because I didn't have any power in the dressing room. I am not saying it was all about me but that was one of the things that was mentioned and is something Ron could have done a bit differently, because there was something missing that day.'

By the time Oldham came to Villa Park, the manager and the players already knew the game was up with regards to the title race. In fairness to them, the team played much better than at Blackburn, but as so often happens when things aren't going your way, the luck is just not with you, as they succumbed to a 1-0 loss in front of their own, dejected supporters.

'We beat Villa at Villa Park to win the league for Manchester United while Fergie was out playing golf!' Oldham manager Joe Royle commented. 'Ron was and still is a big mate of mine. He was absolutely choked after the match.

'Villa were a top side. Even in that game, when Nick Henry scored from the edge of the box as it bobbled in, they battered us. It wasn't very often when we won that I would say, "God, we were lucky there." But on that day, we really rode our luck. They hit the bar, they were all over us, but it just didn't go in for them. Ron, afterwards, was shattered but he shook my hand reluctantly. He was a friend of mine. He knew we needed that win to stay up. We were big mates, but he couldn't bring himself to smile that day, he was absolutely gutted.'

Incredibly, Oldham stayed up on goal difference and Crystal Palace were relegated after Royle's team followed the Villa win with 3-2 and 4-3 home wins over Liverpool and Southampton respectively.

Dean Saunders added, 'The Oldham game was painful. I hit a free kick from about 30 yards, I didn't try to bend it, I just put my foot through it, and it hit the underside of the bar and came out. When I look back at that game, if that had gone in, we would have been cruising. But it came out and, on the day, it wasn't meant to be.'

The trip to QPR was almost inconsequential, merely for pride, and Villa still couldn't stay motivated enough to see out that game as Tony Daley's first-half goal was eventually cancelled out by Les Ferdinand and Bradley Allen. That was it.

'I was absolutely fucking gutted,' Richardson said about missing out on the title, which would have been his third with three different clubs. 'From a purely personal viewpoint, I think I would have been the first player to have won the top division with three different clubs, so for a council house kid like me to have achieved something like that would have been huge. It was a real kick in the bollocks.'

1992/93 season:

League position: 2nd (of 22)

League Cup: fourth round (lost 1-0 at Ipswich Town after a replay)

FA Cup: fourth round (lost 6-5 on penalties at Wimbledon after a replay)

Top scorers: Dean Saunders 16; Dalian Atkinson 13; Garry Parker 9

21

A Trophy at Last, but '82 Boys' Legacy Prevails

'When we got to Wembley, it was actually said between us that we nearly won this and we should have won that … We knew this was our chance to claim some silverware and have something to show for what we did together as a team.'

– Kevin Richardson

EVERY FOUR years Sir Geoff Hurst is inundated with requestss to give interviews and appear on television. Why? Because he is an England legend who had won the World Cup prior to years of subsequent failed attempts to emulate what he and his team-mates achieved in 1966.

Clearly, Hurst is not just any hero or World Cup winner having scored a hat-trick in the Wembley final against West Germany.

If there was an Aston Villa parallel to Hurst it would be Peter Withe after he helped Villa win the First Division title in 1980/81 and then followed that with the only goal in the 1982 European Cup Final triumph over Bayern Munich in Rotterdam.

The thing is, in times of continued success by a national team or club, one trophy and match-winner is lost in the melee of coverage about the next triumph, and the next. Who still talks about Romário and his influence on Brazil at the 1994 World Cup, when the likes of Ronaldo, Rivaldo, Ronaldinho and Neymar have since followed?

Liverpool's many European heroes of the 1970s and '80s such as Terry McDermott, Kenny Dalglish, Alan Kennedy and Bruce Grobbelaar pretty much share equal billing when it comes to their contributions in that period. The feats of the team Steven Gerrard captained in 2005 and the one that Jürgen Klopp managed in 2019 ensures European adulation is not exclusively saved for their heroes of those earlier decades.

As for Villa, Withe and his team-mates from that era are still untouchable and revered by supporters more than 40 years later, which is deserved adulation for the kudos they brought to themselves, the city and their club. They are still so popular with fans because the teams that came after them have won very little, apart from League Cups in 1994 and 1996.

One presumes the 1982 side's legacy would have been diluted somewhat if Graham Taylor's or Ron Atkinson's men had claimed the title in 1990 or 1993 when they were in the mix to do so. Their capitulations earned consolation praise, but ultimately it meant the '82 boys still hold sway as far as Villa's living legends go.

Peter Withe, Jimmy Rimmer, Gary Shaw, captain Dennis Mortimer, Kenny Swain, Ken McNaught, Gordon Cowans, Gary Williams, Des Bremner, Allan Evans, Nigel Spink, Colin Gibson and Tony Morley have mostly been active in the Birmingham area over the years to retell their stories of triumph. Withe, who has lived many years in Australia, less so.

'The legacy from 1982 should be strong and should never be forgotten,' insisted Andy Gray, who Villa sold to local rivals Wolves in 1979. 'To win the league title and then the European Cup a year later is a phenomenal achievement for Aston Villa. Probably something they will never do again, but who knows.

'Yes, had Graham's side or Ron's side gone a step further and won the league, they would have deserved all the credit in the world to be held up there as a great team in Villa's history, but they didn't.'

Results have been kinder to Villa in recent times under Unai Emery's leadership, as he secured Villa's place in the Champions League (or European Cup) for the first time in 41 years in 2024. But prior to his arrival, supporters fed off scraps as far as a winning culture is concerned.

Villa won the League Cup under Atkinson and Brian Little in 1994 and 1996 respectively, but that's been it. They were runners-up in the FA Cup in 2000 and 2015, and second again in the League Cup in 2010 and 2020. Little's team played exciting, adventurous football during his tenure from 1994 to 1998, but the highest Villa finished in the league then was fourth in 1996, back when it didn't lead to Champions League qualification. Martin O'Neill as manager claimed relative success in leading Villa to sixth place in three successive seasons. Maybe that is success to some clubs, especially when a relegation occurs like it did at Villa in 2016, but generally second is not success, never mind sixth.

Most of the Villa players from those two 'nearly' seasons of 1989/90 and 1992/93 still feel frustrated by not being able to go a step further to make history. Taylor's side generally recognise they were a group made up largely of journeymen who combined into a formidably close and vibrant unit, not too unlike the team in 1981 and '82, when there was a void of big names. The 1992/93 side, though, had the names but still couldn't get the job done.

'We definitely over-achieved in our runners-up season, there's no doubt about that,' Kevin Gage said. 'But it was still a missed opportunity having got so close. We missed a few results that ought to have gone our way, but Liverpool probably deserved to win the league with the way they ended that season.

'It's a missed opportunity of course and not many ex-players get to say they won the English league championship. But not many get to say either, "We almost pipped Liverpool for the league title one season and came runners-up." So, it's not all bad.'

Tony Cascarino was of a similar mind that Taylor's Villa team squeezed every ounce of effort out of itself to achieve what they did by pushing Liverpool close in 1990.

'It was a team of over-achievers that absolutely gave their all and were trying to prove themselves at that level after coming through the various levels,' Cascarino said. 'It was a good dressing room full of good lads. But we didn't have any superstars, even though Dwight Yorke was coming through as a youngster.'

Stuart Gray, the captain in 1989/90 said, 'When I see Man City winning the league season after season now, I do get flashbacks about our missed opportunity and still rue that little window against Wimbledon and Coventry that cost us.'

Unlike most of that squad, Derek Mountfield had the consolation of at least retiring with two league title medals in his home cabinet having won the championship in 1985 and 1987 with Everton. But it seems a winners' medal with Villa from that season might have trumped the others given the fact his Everton team was a group of stars like Neville Southall, Kevin Ratcliffe and Kevin Sheedy who won the FA Cup in 1984 then the First Division and European Cup Winners' Cup the following year.

'Any title you win is sweet – we surprised everyone by winning the title in '85 with Everton,' Mountfield commented. 'Nobody expected us to win that year, and nobody expected Villa to win it, so it would have been just as sweet, if not a bit sweeter given where we had been the season before.

'Both teams had a great team spirit. Howard Kendall loved taking the lads away and for Chinese meals and drinks. Graham Taylor was the same, even if it was a couple of nights away at a Pontins or somewhere like that. Both managers really knew how to bond their teams. It was a great shame we couldn't get the job done at Villa as it would have been a magnificent achievement.

'We [Villa in 1990] didn't finish as strong as we would have liked but when you consider where we were the season before, we were so close to winning the title. Although it was a disappointment and we were gutted, we overachieved and had a right good go to qualify for Europe. Several players in our team had been written off like they were finished so it was satisfying to take Liverpool as close as we did. We certainly proved a point even though we didn't win the league.'

Striker and Holte End hero Alan McInally left before Villa's shock campaign in 1989/90, but he did not feel like it was a surprise even though Villa had only just evaded relegation the campaign prior.

'When Graham was initially hoping I would stay, he told me that he was going to bring players in that summer that would make Villa really competitive in the following season,' McInally recalled. 'I ended up leaving and winning the Bundesliga, the Super Cup and reached the semi-finals of the European Cup. But I do think occasionally, "Maybe if I had stayed, we just might have won the league at Villa and that would have been unbelievable." It's all hindsight.

'There is a connection between players and football clubs. I don't really have it at Celtic, I have it at Munich to a certain extent. But when I was at Villa, I had such a happy time. It wasn't difficult for me to leave Celtic as I was neither a Celtic nor a Rangers fan, and there were a few Scottish players at Villa like Neale Cooper and Allan Evans, and Garry Thompson and I got along so well. The whole team had a good bond.

'I don't know what it is, but I still feel the love and the bond every time I come back to Birmingham and Aston Villa. I have always had a good connection with Villa and felt at home there. Players don't always feel that at their clubs.

'If Bayern Munich had not come in for me when they did, I might easily have stayed at Villa for seven or eight years and come close to finishing my career there. Nobody knows, it's ifs and buts, but it could have happened.

'What I do know, though, is I was so lucky to be a Holte End hero in my brief stay at Villa. Every time I put my head on the pillow at night, I feel blessed that the Villa fans still sing that song, "Spinksy and Birchy, Alan McInally ..." I only hope Birchy can hear it.'

One event that cheered the Villa supporters going into the 1993/94 season was the re-signing of 1982 Rotterdam hero Gordon Cowans, who was coming back for a third spell at the club after Atkinson had sold him to Blackburn, only to then watch Cowans orchestrate the match at Ewood Park that drove one of the final nails into Villa's failed title bid.

'I sold Sid for £175,000 but was happy to bring him back to help bolster our squad as he was free, we knew him well, he loved the Villa, and we were in Europe and another Englishman was useful with the quota system,' Atkinson said. 'There was nothing to lose. I remember him playing against Slovan Bratislava and he was brilliant.

'We still ended up getting 40 grand for him from Derby. It became a standing joke between me and Sid, "Go and have a year there and come back again!"'

The major addition of that 1993 summer, though, was Andy Townsend from Chelsea, as the manager showed yet again that he was capable of bringing in the best talent around.

'I still had it in mind,' said Big Ron, 'that he could play left-sided [after Paul Mortimer and Garry Parker had not worked out in that position, with Parker preferring a central role]. Andy had a good presence about him and could play in the middle also.'

The 1993/94 league and European campaigns were something of an anti-climax after the highs of the previous season, as Villa finished tenth and exited the UEFA Cup in the second round to Deportivo La Coruña. The 1993/94 season was all about the League Cup.

Tony Daley, one of the most electrifying entertainers that Villa Park has seen down the years with his rapid pace on the flanks, was disappointed at finishing as a league championship runner-up in both 1990 and 1993. However, he made his peace with history, but only because he was able to win the League Cup under Atkinson.

'If we never won the League Cup in '94, I would have badly regretted not winning the league,' Daley said. 'That cup win was like a consolation for me that I was finally able to win something with Villa.'

Skipper Kevin Richardson felt all the previous near-misses and failures to get over the line in title run-ins or key cup games motivated that 3-1 Wembley victory over Manchester United in '94. The win not only handed Villa their first trophy in 11 years, since winning the European Super Cup, but also prevented United from maintaining their bid for a treble. Alex Ferguson's team had to make do with a mere double instead.

'We should have won a lot more, especially in my time under Big Ron,' Richardson commented. 'We all recognised that as a group of players. So, when we got to Wembley, it was actually said between us that we nearly won this and we should have won that. We gave up the league title the season before, if that's the right phrase, we didn't beat Liverpool and Oldham in FA Cup quarter-finals. We lost to Bolton in the last 16 of the FA Cup that season. We knew this was our chance to claim some silverware and have something to show for what we did together as a team. And we did it.

'It would have been interesting to get into some players' minds about whether they really believed we could beat Man U. But on the day, we worked really hard for each other and got the job done. I think our desire was more than theirs on that day.'

Villa really had to earn that trophy. After 1-0 wins in both legs against fierce rivals Birmingham City, they went to Sunderland and won 4-1 despite being under attack for much of the game.

'We won comfortably according to the score, but Bozzy kept us in the game,' Atkinson recalled. 'We broke away four times and scored four wonder goals, while Bozzy was pulling saves off like you couldn't believe. He beat them on his own.'

One Sunderland scribe wrote on the Roker Report website, 'Bosnich defied not only the laws of gravity but also physics and other branches of science into the bargain. His human octopus-like display was to frustrate us time and time again as we relentlessly pounded the Villa goal … He produced the most incredible display of goalkeeping I've ever witnessed at Roker Park.'

That was Bosnich's breakthrough game and Big Ron observed another youngster whose performance he acted on that night: Black Cats winger Martin Smith, who had been dubbed the 'Son of Pelé' by a Sunderland fanzine. Smith tore apart Villa's usually reliable right-back Earl Barrett.

'Ryan Giggs reckoned Earl was the hardest defender he ever played against, but Martin Smith flew past him like he wasn't there,' Atkinson revealed. 'I said to Mick Buxton after the game, "I'll give you a million quid for your winger now!" But it never really became too much of a thing as he had a few injury troubles and he ended up going to Huddersfield.'

Villa were then drawn at Arsenal, where they had won 2-1 in the league just three weeks earlier. It was said that the Gunners were determined to avenge that defeat, yet they lost again, this time to a single goal from Dalian Atkinson. The tough challenges kept coming for Villa as their next draw in the quarter-finals was Tottenham away, where they managed a 2-1 victory after a winner from Barrett, who scored one of his two goals for the club in his 150 appearances.

It then appeared Villa had been handed the kinder semi-final against Tranmere Rovers from the second tier. United, meantime, were drawn against Sheffield Wednesday, who had the likes of Chris Waddle, Des Walker, Carlton Palmer, David Hirst and Mark Bright in their ranks. United made light of the Owls with 1-0 and 4-1 wins to set up a final showdown with Villa, but only after they overcame one of the most thrilling semi-finals of the generation in front of a crowd of 40,593, which created one of *the* greatest atmospheres ever known at Villa Park.

Rovers were leading 3-0 in the first leg at Prenton Park and it looked as though Villa's cup run was about to end, only for Dalian Atkinson to stab home a consolation goal in the dying seconds that kept the semi-final alive.

Atkinson again saved Villa at home with an 88th-minute goal that levelled the aggregate score at 4-4, which it remained after extra time, forcing the tie into penalties.

Atkinson, though, had so nearly clinched the win in the last minute of extra time after one of his signature mazy dribbles that would have been as good as his goal at Wimbledon had he managed to find the net at the end of it.

Villa won the penalty shoot-out 5-4 but only after more incredible drama.

Dean Saunders and Shaun Teale both scored, equalised each time by Tranmere, then Villa went 3-2 up with the third kick – taken by 19-year-old substitute Graham Fenton, in just his second senior appearance for the club.

Ged Brannan saw his spot kick saved by Mark Bosnich, giving Villa the advantage, then Dalian Atkinson scored and Tranmere were on target again to make it 4-3.

Another rookie substitute, Ugo Ehiogu, had the chance to win it for Villa but hit the bar, before John

Aldridge scored to equalise at 4-4 and take the shoot-out to sudden death, where Kevin Richardson shot over and gave the visitors a kick for victory.

Bosnich came up trumps again with a save from Liam O'Brien, before Tony Daley scored Villa's seventh and Ian Nolan then had to find the net for Tranmere to keep his team in it.

Nolan couldn't do what was necessary. Bosnich made his third save of the shoot-out and Ron Atkinson's men were heading to Wembley.

With Villa through to meet United, Atkinson's former club where he won the FA Cup twice as manager, the scene was set for one last hurrah towards silverware. But standing in their way was a great team, and still improving formidably.

Sealey, Parker, Irwin, Bruce, Pallister, Keane, Kanchelskis, Ince, Cantona, Hughes and Giggs was the Red Devils' line-up.

When Villa's side was announced there was great shock among the supporters at Wembley and those watching at home that Big Ron had selected Fenton over the experienced options of Ray Houghton and Garry Parker, while Steve Staunton played with an injured groin, opting for a starting XI of Bosnich, Barrett, Staunton,

Teale, McGrath, Richardson, Fenton, Townsend, Saunders, Atkinson and Daley.

'I looked at Man United and thought we have got to have some physical presence in there,' Big Ron explained. 'Fenton had been on loan at West Brom and Leicester and I'd seen him play a few reserves games and I thought, "He looks like he's ready." I wanted the three most physical midfield players and they were Andy [Townsend], Richo and young Fenton. Garry Parker was brilliant about it. I had my team talk before the final and named the side and then said to the XI, you can go, and same to the subs. Then I looked at the other lads who weren't going to be on the bench and said, "Sorry lads, you've missed out this time. But remember how this feels and make sure you don't miss out next time." Then I asked Garry to look after them and he was brilliant at consoling them and geeing them up and keeping their spirits up. Top pro was Garry.'

Dalian Atkinson and Dean Saunders put Villa 2-0 up by the 75th minute and only a goal by Mark Hughes in the 83rd created late tension in the Villa camp, until Saunders added a last-minute third from the penalty spot. Andrei Kanchelskis was also sent off for United to cap off a nightmare final for them.

At last Villa had a trophy again, even though it wasn't the league.

Saunders was one of the manager's golden boys and, days after the final, he wasted no time in knocking on the manager's door for an improved contract.

Saunders recalled, 'We came second the previous season when I scored 17 goals, then we won the cup the season after, so I thought this is the right time to ask for the pay rise he'd promised me when I signed. I knocked on his door and reminded him of our conversation:

'"Gaffer, you said if I do well, you'd put my wages back to the way they were at Liverpool."

'"Yeah, carry on …"

'"Well, I know things aren't all down to me, but we were mid-table when I got here and then we went to top, I've scored 30-odd goals, we're in Europe so the club is making more money, we've won a cup …"

'"This is Aston Villa – we're expected to do that. What else?"

'"I won player of the year."

'"I never voted for you! Now get out!" [Saunders laughs].

'I never did get paid as much as when I was at Liverpool, but Ron gave me the pay rise eventually.

That was Ron, he was brilliant, and I still play golf with him. I loved playing for him.'

Most of the Villa players loved Atkinson, but unfortunately for him his greatest weakness was his inability to play up to chairman Doug Ellis's ego. Both had huge egos and there was only ever one winner at Aston Villa whenever there was a clash. There was a common feeling within the corridors of power at Villa that once Big Ron's luck ran out in terms of results, as it usually does for all football managers at one time, Ellis would strike.

Despite the Wembley triumph, Villa had ended the 1993/94 league campaign in horrible form, winning just two of their last 12 games and losing eight. Two of those defeats came in the last three games and were 5-1 and 4-1 hammerings at Newcastle and Southampton respectively. The Kevin Keegan feelgood factor was being felt at St James' Park, while the player who Atkinson had once considered bidding for, Matt Le Tissier, scored twice in that Southampton game. An otherwise disappointing climax to the season was momentarily stalled in the final match as Villa beat Liverpool 2-1 courtesy of two Dwight Yorke goals. It was an emotional day at Villa Park as the famous old Holte End was to be demolished three days later with plans to replace it with seating. Yorke and his team-mates gave the great old stand a fitting send-off.

The 1994/95 season followed in a similar pattern. By 9 November, Atkinson's team had won just two league matches and slipped to 19th in the table, which persuaded Ellis to terminate Atkinson's contract. It had certainly been a horror run of league results for Villa, but there was still an element of shock among the fans who mostly seemed to think he deserved more time to turn things around, after three mostly good years and a cup win under his management. But Ellis was not nicknamed 'Deadly' for nothing. The final nail for Atkinson was a defeat at Wimbledon – who else – that almost became comical it was so bad. After an early Warren Barton penalty, Villa fought back to take a 3-1 lead with half an hour remaining. But three late Wimbledon goals shattered Villa and ultimately did for Atkinson as Villa boss.

He was sacked the next day after the miserable loss at Selhurst Park. Ellis had first canvassed the opinions of board members to see if they agreed it was the right time for Big Ron to go. They were unanimous, but at that time, there was nobody brave enough to disagree with Ellis, who was pretty much a one-man supremo.

Villa had taken just one point from a possible 24 in the league, while also exiting the UEFA Cup to Turkish outfit Trabzonspor.

The divide that had increased in the relationship between Ellis and Atkinson certainly influenced the decision to fire Atkinson and Ellis even admitted as much in his subsequent autobiography. He said had Atkinson been more amenable to discuss the slide by the team, they might have been able to work together to rectify matters. However, Ellis felt he was more likely to see his manager on television discussing the plight of other clubs.

'I wouldn't have wanted to get on the wrong side of Doug because he could be quite ruthless,' Tony Cascarino said, 'but he would do it in a quiet way. Ken Bates at Chelsea would just tell you to "fuck off".'

The shining light for Atkinson of his final Villa campaign had been a UEFA Cup triumph over Inter Milan, who had the likes of Dennis Bergkamp, Rubén Sosa and Giuseppe Bergomi in their team. New signing Phil King converted the winning penalty in a shoot-out after he strode up to the penalty spot whistling. Villa tied Inter 1-1 on aggregate and then won 4-3 on penalties.

Skipper Kevin Richardson felt shattered by Atkinson's sacking and wondered whether all the players had been doing as much as they possibly could to have turned results around.

'If you have a few players that think, "It's OK, we can just turn up and win," it's a hard mentality to dig yourselves out of when the opponents are on top,' he said. 'Unless all 11 players are pulling in the same direction, it can be tough going.'

Atkinson was never going to receive more time to improve results from Ellis because the owner had been biding his time to remove him. The negative history had been slowly building.

Ellis later described the relationship between himself and Atkinson as 'distant' and said they never did share the close working relationship that he had wanted. Ellis took a dim view of Atkinson's social behaviour after matches and described some of his acquaintances as 'undesirables'. Others who were close to both men felt the chairman was a little jealous of Atkinson's social circle and longed to be part of it.

Ellis blamed Atkinson for Villa not signing Andy Cole from Bristol City after the striker had been offered for £1.2m. Ellis claimed he tried to reach Atkinson but could not and the deal was lost. The chairman never liked how Atkinson failed to keep him up to speed with team and club business and he had to read about it in the media instead.

Ellis claimed he advised Atkinson that the squad needed freshening up ahead of the 1994/95 campaign, yet Atkinson disagreed and maintained the squad was good to go again and be a top-six team. His only signings that summer had been Nii Lamptey, Phil King and John Fashanu.

Ellis was especially uncomfortable with Fashanu's apparent commitments off the field with UNICEF and the TV show *Gladiators*, which meant he negotiated times when he didn't have to train midweek. Ellis later conceded that Fashanu was the most intelligent footballer he had ever dealt with and his ability for articulate negotiation was 'unsurpassed'.

Fashanu was injured while at Villa, which ended his career. Villa settled with him by paying an *ex gratia* payment of £250,000, while the club claimed the insurance fee of £1.3m, which was pretty much the transfer fee they had paid for him.

Ellis also didn't like how Atkinson agreed the purchase of Dean Saunders for £2.5m from Liverpool and felt there was a better deal to be had. Subsequently, Ellis became involved and was smug in his subsequent conversation with Atkinson when he revealed that the player had been purchased, for £2.3m. It resembled the standoff over transfer control between Ellis and another Ron, Saunders, almost 20 years earlier when Saunders agreed his first signing with former club Manchester City. Frank Carrodus was the player on that occasion.

Secretary Steve Stride felt Big Ron never approached his relationship with Ellis in the right way and it cost him dearly in the end. Whereas Graham Taylor had full control over team matters and dealt with Ellis with an authority that suggested to the chairman that he should dare not interfere, he also had the diplomacy to indulge the chairman at times and play to his ego. That wasn't Atkinson's style.

'Doug had Jo [Vengloš] who he controlled and now he had Ron who was uncontrollable,' Stride said. 'Doug was always limited in his praise towards Ron because he was never front and centre like Ron, which was where he wanted to be. That's why it all ended messily. Doug bided his time and waited for the moment to sack Ron, after the infamous Wimbledon result.

'Ron would think nothing of telling the chairman to "fuck off", and in front of people. I used to think to myself, "Don't do that Ron," or "Don't say those things Ron," because ultimately Doug was the real boss and Ron was only in charge of the team. I knew how it made Doug feel and he was storing up all those times that Ron belittled him. He was always going to have his revenge one day, which he did.

'I was disappointed when Ron left because we were signing good players and the team was performing well most of the time. But when you abuse the chairman, it's going to come back to bite you and in some ways, I understood why Doug got rid of Ron as he was his boss and shouldn't be listening to him telling him to "fuck off". But it was a shame.'

Ellis had always verbally agreed a mutually acceptable severance package with managers he fired, according to Stride. Atkinson, though, was the first who wanted more and required further negotiation.

'Ron's biggest flaw was that he always wanted to be the big-time Charlie and could speak down to people but because he didn't play at a very high grade himself it seemed a bit odd at times,' Cascarino added. 'He'd say things on the golf course like, "You go and play off the ladies' tees." And you can imagine him getting through his time at Man United being like that, all gobby and cocky, but sometimes it didn't do him any good.'

The biggest loser, ultimately, was Aston Villa Football Club and its supporters. The three years and more under Atkinson had been exciting: high-profile players wanted to sign for the club and often did; the football was mostly vibrant and often produced good results, until the last few months. All good things come to an end, though. Where one door closes, another opens and Holte End hero Brian Little succeeded Atkinson. In time, after a renovation of Atkinson's squad, Little would also produce vibrant football and even won another League Cup, in 1996. He reached an FA Cup semi-final in 1996 and finished fourth the same year. But he was also unable to win the league like Atkinson, Taylor or any of his subsequent successors to this very day. At the time of writing, Unai Emery is re-energising the club and raising fans' expectations to heights not seen for 40 years. But for now, despite the near misses over the years, nobody ever remembers second and therefore those great champions of 1981 and 1982 still reign supreme.

1993/94 season:

League position: 10th (of 22)

League Cup: winners (beat Manchester United 3-1 at Wembley)

FA Cup: fifth round (lost 1-0 at Bolton Wanderers)

UEFA Cup: second round (lost 2-1 on aggregate to Deportivo La Coruña)

Top scorers: Dean Saunders 18; Dalian Atkinson 15; Kevin Richardson 7

1994/95 season:

League position: 18th (of 22, when four were relegated)

League Cup: fourth round (lost 4-1 at Crystal Palace)

FA Cup: fourth round (lost 1-0 at Manchester City)

UEFA Cup: second round (lost on away goals rule to Trabzonspor)

Top scorers: Dean Saunders 17; Dwight Yorke 8; Dalian Atkinson 7

Acknowledgements

THANK YOU to the following for their support or who gave their time to be interviewed:

Ron Atkinson, especially, as his honest and vivid memories over lunch at the Barnt Green Inn added great depth to this memoir, Liam Brady, Tony Cascarino, Tony Daley, Allan Evans, Kevin Gage, Bobby Gould, Andy Gray (the Scottish one!), Stuart Gray, Ray Houghton, Martin Keown, Alan McInally, Derek Mountfield, Ian Ormondroyd, David Platt, Kevin Richardson, Joe Royle, Dean Saunders, Graeme Souness, Steve Stride, Garry Thompson, and also Dwight Yorke for his interview and for supplying the foreword. By the way, Dwight was my very first interviewee back in 1994 when I spoke to him in my Austin Maestro at Bodymoor Heath for a Birmingham newspaper! He has remained helpful and supportive ever since, so thanks my friend.

Bibliography

Books:

Ellis, H.D., *Deadly Doug, Behind the Scenes at Aston Villa FC* (John Blake Publishing, 2005)

McGrath, P., *Back from the Brink* (Arrow Books, 2006)

Platt, D., *Achieving the Goal* (Richard Cohen Books, 1995)

Souness, G., *Football: My Life, My Passion* (Headline, 2017)

Taylor, G., *In his Own Words* (Peloton Publishing, 2017)

Websites:

The English National Football Archive

Wikipedia